Advanced NLP Strategies for Changing Minds

Shlomo Vaknin
Erickson Institute

Disclaimer

This material is not intended to substitute for professional medical advice or clinical training. It is intended to by used by practitioners within their scope of practice and competence. It is the responsibility of the reader to know what training, certification, or licensure they need in order to utilize the techniques disclosed in this book. The author disclaims all warranties, either express or implied, including fitness for a particular purpose. The author does not warrant that this book can be relied upon for full applicability to any purpose or situation. Thus, the author is not responsible for any errors or omissions or for the results obtained from the use of this information. The author makes no representation or warranties, express or implied. In no event shall the author, any contributors or editors, or anyone referenced as a source or authority be liable for any claims or damages (including, without limitation, direct, incidental and consequential damages, personal injury/wrongful death, lost profits, resulting from the use of or inability to use this book, whether based on warranty, contract, tort, or any other legal theory, and whether or not the author is advised of the possibility of such damages). The author is not liable for any personal injury, including death, caused by your use or misuse of this book.

Advanced NLP Strategies for Changing Minds

Shlomo Vaknin
Erickson Institute

Advanced NLP Strategies for Changing Minds

ISBN: 9788087518304

Manufactured in the United States of America.

A Free Six-Hour Audio-Course

If you bought this book and you're new to NLP, you're entitled to a free six-hour audiobook designed specifically for beginners, focusing on the essentials. To get your free audiobook, please contact Ben at help@ericks.org

Other Books by the Author

- **The BIG Book of NLP, Expanded**: 350+ Techniques, Patterns & Strategies of Neuro Linguistic Programming
- **500 Practical NLP Forms, Templates & Worksheets**: Ready-to-Use Essential Tools for Therapy, Coaching and Training
- **Fear of Rejection**: NLP Tools You Can Use
- **Porn Addiction**: Self-Therapy Workbook (A Step by Step Protocol for Regaining Control)
- A Short Guide to **Self-Motivation**
- NLP: The **57 Meta-Programs**

- **Advanced NLP Techniques** for Therapists & Coaches
- **The Big Book of Self-Analysis:** Discover Your Untapped Potential
- **Our Most Effective Hypnotic Scripts** (Book Series)
- **NLP Forms & Templates** (single worksheet in multiple copies - booklets)

Contents

Introduction

This book is an advanced, modern NLP manual for therapists and coaches who want to expand and update their use of Neuro Linguistic Programming.

The concepts and methods we describe come from extensive experience in the field with a broad variety of clients. This book takes on three unique training challenges: First, to provide techniques in the context of the work. For example, the techniques are described in terms of how they link one phase of your work with the next; secondly, to provide very condensed techniques that target a very specific purpose and moment in the work; and... thirdly, to provide fundamental understandings about Neuro Linguistic Programming that will improve your ability to develop methods, customize your approach to the individual client, and improvise. I'd like to point out some special qualities of this book:

1) **Modern:** This book takes into account the great progress in psychology and psychotherapy that has taken place since Neuro Linguistic Programming was first developed. This work consciously takes up the challenge of using well-grounded information from the mental health field and the research that supports it, while standing on the firmest assumptions and methods of Neuro Linguistic Programming.

NLP largely began by modeling psychotherapists who mystified their field with their unique gifts and skills. But, forty years later, psychotherapy innovations and research have taken great steps. Today, NLP is ready for a global review that exclusively brings together fully-grounded understanding with the catalytic insights that transform practitioners into masters. I hope you find that this work fulfills that mission.

2) **Clear:** I made every effort to describe the ideas and methods in a very clear, direct way.

3) **Advanced:** This book plunges the reader directly into NLP application and modern theory, without plodding through the basics of Neuro Linguistic Programming. The focus is on taking you to a new level of proficiency. We provide the techniques in terms that people with some experience will appreciate. Rather than only providing step-by-step descriptions, we chose this time to show the reader **nuances and choices** that enhance the reader's capacity for customizing and improvising.

A good example of this is in the rapport-building patterns here. Rather than the detailed and classic rapport building description, such as the one in The Big Book of NLP, the rapport patterns in this book are more focused and nuanced, building on your core, classic NLP rapport skills. Another example is the **Positive Contribution Experience**, in which the therapist consistently responds as if the client can do no wrong. Unlike a classic NLP pattern, this is an approach with numerous guidelines and ways of responding creatively. It takes on an almost chess-like quality.

The approach is supported by modern knowledge such as **Secure Base Priming**. It is presented in the context of the larger approach to therapy, along with methods such as **The Honored Values Elicitation Experience**, which leverages the client's contributions and values.

4) **Big picture aspect:** This book takes the approach of holistically connecting all points of a healing relationship rather than simply collecting techniques. For example, each section of the book deals with a phase of the relationship and the work required. Rather than only providing techniques in steps, many of the entries provide *ingredients* and *guidance* for successful coaching and therapy.

This is designed to help you leverage and integrate your existing knowledge of Neuro Linguistic Programming and other successful approaches (you noticed the presupposition in the last sentence, didn't you?). Some of the material provides simple elements that might be thought of as being *fragments* of NLP patterns. We offer them because they can comprise critical turning points for moments or phases in therapy. By focusing at that level of detail, we can spend time on some of the more subtle nuances of technique. Such nuances can, for example, help you maintain momentum in the therapy or coaching process. Much as the same DNA appears in every organ, such nuances can appear in many NLP techniques. We refer to this kind of skill development as *"granular embedding."*

5) **Techniques for you AND your clients:** We will also provide a good number of straightforward, simple techniques. You can teach many of these directly to your clients. Patterns such as the **Compelling Speech** patterns and the **Communication Improvement** patterns are good examples. Some of these are of the more *granular* variety that integrates well into larger patterns or approaches.

Preparing for Change Work

For your own and your client's sake, it may be beneficial to emphasize at some point throughout your collaboration that, even after the two of you identify the sources of an issue, work is required to modify patterns and behaviors. Your theoretical perspective will inform your definition of the change process. Some clinicians feel that higher self-awareness and remedial experiences can emerge as your clients engage in actions they have avoided or never considered, allowing them to perceive more possibilities. Depending on your theoretical views, reality testing leads to further corrective experiences, which you may refer to as "working through" or "repeated exposure." What a client wants to hear is that he is working on himself and that he is the agent shaping his destiny. "Our focus is on you, on enabling you to better focus on your strengths and opportunities for improvement so that you may recognize the sources of your patterns and choose options that will best utilize your talents."

Your theoretical views will assist you in making decisions. For example, if you use a cognitive method that focuses on modifying thoughts and actions, you would assess progress by looking at your client's maladaptive and adaptive thought processes. More explicitly, behavioral approaches to client change will look for new, healthy activities as an indicator of change, with an emphasis on identifying and fostering positive actions. Holistic techniques, with their emphasis on intrapersonal and interpersonal relationships, will seek transformation in the form of fewer internal issues, resolution of painful experiences, and more fulfilling personal endeavors. Humanistic or experiential methods of therapy anticipate changes in enhanced emotional awareness, more real experiences, and a better sense of personal identity.

Structural approaches to change will expect improvement in places where there is rigid enmeshment inside or, alternatively, far separation from social systems. Practitioners who combine physiological interventions with strategies will almost certainly be looking for changes in wellness practices and improvements in mind-body awareness. People who work with people from different cultures and who are also feminists and multicultural will be on the lookout for ways to help their clients adapt to societal forces like prejudice and oppressive cultural values and norms.

Current Reality

It is essential to be aware of what is going on in the here and now in order to respond effectively and flexibly to one's experiences.

Most people are so preoccupied with their feelings, memories, body sensations, fears, and ruminations that they fail to see the possibilities for living in accordance with their values that are all around them all the time.

People may have difficulty recognizing what they are thinking or feeling, despite the fact that their actions may be influenced by these thoughts and feelings. People who act "mindlessly" respond to their thoughts in an automatic, unconscious way, as though they have no knowledge of the thoughts or experiences that prompted them.

The vast majority of our thoughts are based on previous events or future forecasts, and we tend to focus on the past when making decisions.

These personal encounters have a way of seizing our attention and removing us from the present moment and the rest of the world. To illustrate the point, let's look at just one example of mindless activity.

In the past, have you ever driven or walked back to your destination only to discover that you had no idea how you got there? Otherwise, you would have been involved in an accident if you were driving and responding to stop signs and other vehicles. Choosing which bus or train to ride, where to sit, and when to get off were all options if you used public transportation. As a result, you didn't even realize how much you were "languaging" (thinking and enforcing rules).

The linguistic processes of making decisions and following rules were operating at some level, but you were not in direct contact with them during the moment. It's possible that you were daydreaming about dinner while driving–to the point that it felt like you were already home and preparing it. Even though the future is not here and now, it can be experienced in the here and now using this method. In the same way, you may have been thinking about a chat you had with your boss earlier in the day as you sat on the train. Even if it has already happened, the past lives on in the here and now.

This may seem like a benign example, but it illustrates the perils of failing to pay attention to our own feelings and the events taking place around us. Suicide attempts, self-harm, and substance addiction are just a few of the potentially life-threatening activities that clients may engage in while in treatment. Even in its mildest and least harmful manifestations, a loss of awareness of the here and now can have a negative impact. Losing the chance to receive touch reinforcement as a result of engaging in desired activities is particularly relevant in this case. When a person is substantially disconnected from his experiences and the world around him, it is difficult to be aware of and earn reinforcement from values-consistent activities.

Therapists trained in NLP advocate for clients to engage in regular, nonjudgmental communication with themselves and the world around them rather than just going through the motions of life.

When a client is more aware of the present moment, he or she will be better able to behave in accordance with the values he or she chooses to live by.

It is recommended that clients should not attempt to assess the events they are observing or describing, but rather simply note and explain them. Awareness is deliberately fostered with the goal of fostering a position from which the client may see his thoughts, feelings, and other intimate happenings in a nonjudgmental way. In this way, the customer may observe how values-based actions are put into practice.

Ericksonian and NLP approaches to being in the present require following a rule that prescribes careful attention to the immediate present environment in order to increase the regulatory effects of this environment on behavior and reduce the typical levels of function transformation. In the long run, if this rule is followed consistently, the person's ability to discern components of his environment that may have been less conspicuous previously but that may be crucial to his valued goals will likely rise (for example, his own behavior and that of others in everyday social interactions).

> The NLP overall strategy relies heavily on the gradual weakening of the regulatory effects of language on behavior, which can be achieved through consistent adherence to this rule.

The benefits of being present may grow stronger over time if they are recognized and practiced on a daily basis.

Resistance

Resistance exists in therapy on a regular basis, much like weather. Like the weather, you can become upset, be dissatisfied, complain, rant, take it personally, and feel horrible, but the snow, sun, and wind will keep on coming no matter how you react to it. A raincoat may be necessary from time to time.

> Resisting isn't a personal attack; neither is the weather. It's hard to change people's ways, especially when they're in pain; they're afraid and stubborn.

Don't be critical of your client's reluctance to try a new technique. If a customer feels threatened, she will need to defend herself. She will be more receptive to your suggestions if she feels understood. You begin, "You didn't enjoy the diary writing. What's going on?" Regardless of whether it's a book, meditation, a recommendation, behavior tracking, paying attention to dreams, exercise, or anything else, the goal is to improve one's well-being. "I realize that you want to feel better, but change is hard," you can explain further. If we can come up with anything you wish to follow, then let's try it."

Go for it! Customize your methods in conjunction with your customers. In order to help you get your ideas and feelings out of your head and onto paper in between our sessions, we devised journal writing. But if you don't write, it won't help. Let's go over it in terms of what you want to accomplish. Afterwards, we'll be able to determine if trying it again is worth your time.

Another way to approach journal writing is to say, "It's evident that you're having a hard time with this topic."How did you feel about writing in your journal at the time? Now, with this information, we'll be able to figure out what works and what doesn't. When you tried to implement our plan, what happened?"

When a technique is effective, it is because the client understands it, believes in it, and is willing to participate in it.

Tossing notebooks, charts, exercises, and other tactics into therapy in the hope that one of them will stick is at best superficial and, at worst, can destroy the connection.

Your time is being wasted if you pursue a technique without first dealing with the client's reluctance. If your tactics don't stem directly from your client's problem, build on her strengths, and are clearly presented to her, you're wasting your time and your client's. All of these conditions can only be met in the context of a solid therapeutic partnership. They fail if they don't. We also encourage you to keep up with new methodologies for specific populations and issues, as it is easy to get familiar with distinctive methods.

> When you establish rapport, you lower the client's resistance.

In order to build rapport, you must be able to empathize with the other person's feelings. Observe how people sit or stand, hold their heads and bodies, and use their words and voices in a subtle way to copy them. As a result, you'll feel more comfortable conversing with the other individual.

As a doctor, you can't even begin to understand how terrified a patient in a wheelchair is unless you enter into their "state" and experience what they are going through. Sit next to them when you converse, so you're both on the same level in terms of height. Explore how it might make you feel to be unable to get up and walk away; consider why they are in the hospital and how their sensations might be accompanied by a diagnosis. If the patient was transferred from a ward to a new department without notice or explanation, think about the uncertainty they may be experiencing. In addition, think about what it would be like to initially enter your department. Perhaps one day you will spend a few minutes entering the building from the main entrance and taking in everything you can. Is there anything that could make you worried or uncomfortable if you were unfamiliar with the surroundings? Is there anything that would make you more at ease?

> When developing rapport, it's important to match the other person's energy level.

It's impossible to build rapport with someone who is irate or enraged by talking to them slowly and quietly. Once you've established rapport, you may progressively slow things down and "guide" them to a calmer state by matching the intensity level without aggressiveness or using threatening language.

Obviously, you don't want to match exactly what someone is feeling, so choose certain elements that will help you bring them out of their unpleasant condition. Anger can't be dealt with through retaliation. A radiographer who mastered the art of building rapport employed this method to great effect in his case study, Richard's Story.

Learning how to build rapport with your patients could be one of the most valuable skills you can learn. Increasing your awareness of when you are in and out of rapport can help you receive the information you need to treat your patient effectively, so we encourage you to do the same for yourself in order to get the results you want even faster.

Practice Rapport With Other Professionals

Invite a coworker to join you on a workout. Therefore, the activity is designed to demonstrate how employing rapport may influence how you feel in any situation. Therefore, explain the basics of rapport to them.

Discuss an issue that is at least a little contentious.

Start a conversation about it with your coworker and express your agreement with what they have to say. When conversing, intentionally mismatch your coworker to avoid being out of sync. Do not be afraid to move around. If they are talking in a high tone, lower your voice; if they are sitting with their legs crossed and leaning back, uncross them.

A couple more minutes of talking might be appropriate.

You might begin to create rapport with the other person by changing your point of view at a convenient time.

A couple more minutes of talking might be appropriate.

Finally, spend some time agreeing and creating rapport with the other person. Let's stop the chit-chat.

Describe how you felt during each "section" of the discussion.

Take a few minutes to think about how this might apply to your own work. For example, while positioning a patient for imaging or setting up a clean trolley, consider whether or not you and your patient are on speaking terms, and then consider what you could do to restore that connection when the conditions are less than ideal, such as while talking with someone who is lying on a hospital bed.

Content & Context

We tend to tell ourselves stories about who we are as we go through life. Coherence is something we all want as people. It's human nature to seek evidence that supports our self-conceptualizations and to ignore that which does not support them.

> To predict and manage our behavior, we need a consistent self-image that integrates all our experiences, but we can get attracted to or engaged in certain events over others.

The range of possible behaviors we can engage in can be restricted if we have a rigid, literal commitment to our conceptualized self, or self-as-content. It is common for many clients who have a strong sense of attachment to a conceptualized self to acquire an attachment to the assumption that their difficulties govern their lives at the expense of living in accordance with the values they hold dear.

An example of this would be a client who has constructed an image of himself as a high-achieving individual. In his relentless pursuit of excellence, he never stops to consider whether he appreciates the projects he accepts or the accolades he receives as an achiever. It's not that achieving goals is a bad thing, but for this client, none of his actions are tied to anything that he considers valuable. It's not uncommon for him to reveal his fear of failing to his therapist.

Achieving a goal, being the first to finish a project, or being the greatest at your job is the only time he feels good about himself. For some reason, when he isn't able to get his hands on the latest electrical item, he is afraid that his supervisor will think that he is being cheap. Afraid of having to face the fact that he isn't flawless, he will go to great measures to hide his mistakes by lying and covering them up. It's a highly planned existence that doesn't feel vital for a long time because of his idea of himself as ambitious and ideal.

A fatigued client like this is more likely to seek treatment during times of crisis (such as an impending divorce, job layoff, or financial difficulties), despite having all of the "things" they desire but feeling disconnected from others around them.

NLP therapists work to cultivate a transcendent sense of self, or self-as-context, in contrast to a concentration on self-as-content. It is possible to get perspective on one's own experiences by just watching and recounting them without judgment.

Through the use of relational frames such as I-you, now-then, and here-there, we are able to establish an expanded sense of self as a locus or perspective in human language. Taking this view can assist clients in seeing that their private experiences don't define, threaten, or control them, and that they can be present in the flow of their experiences rather than being emotionally invested in or attached to any one of them.

> An important aspect of NLP is the use of metaphors and experiential procedures to help people develop a deeper understanding of themselves in their own context.

This open, defused, transcendent sense of self is a lot more likely to see values-consistent behavior as reinforcing and meaningful from this point of view than someone who doesn't have this sense of self.

NLP for Therapy

If NLP is a collection of techniques that were modeled from people who didn't do NLP, then isn't NLP just a bag of other people's techniques? It may sound like it at first, but the right answer is:

No, definitely not.

Let's put the bag of techniques in the closet for a moment and look at what's left. We have the *presuppositions*, the deconstruction of the cognitive process into *sense modalities*, and we have a strong philosophy and approach to *modeling excellence*. But wait...

- The presuppositions are successful ideas from successful people;
- the deconstruction of cognitive processes is done in various ways in cognitive psychotherapy;
- and everybody knows you can learn a lot about how to do something from people who already know how to do it.

Isn't NLP just a bushel of truisms and other people's skills? No, definitely not. Let's put the bushel truisms and other people's skills in the closet with the bag. Well, now all that's left is a lot of people promoting training with big promises. **Is NLP just a blast of hot air?**

Yet again: No, definitely not.

Let's put the blast of hot air in with the bushel and the bag. Now all that's left is the *spirit* of Neuro Linguistic Programming. That is, a spirited pursuit of understanding and techniques that produce results. This is a force for innovation and integration that has been behind all major progress in civilization and technology. **But that isn't unique to Neuro Linguistic Programming.** Does that mean there's nothing left? You would not be surprised by our answer:

No, definitely not.

Let's put the spirit of innovation and integration into the closet with the bag, the bushel, and the blast. My, you have some amazing things in your closet! Even if the hot air drifts out, you can always use NLP to put it back and become a good sales person or advocate for your services. *Even if someone took away the bag of techniques, the spirit and philosophy would create more.*

For the purposes of this book, we would like to think of NLP as integration and innovation directed toward excellence, success, and healing.

Also, it is based on fundamental philosophical ideas. This has brought useful **exemplars** (people who we model), knowledge and experience together in service of its goals (or outcomes). From these spring techniques, crafted into forms of training that propagate them effectively. Many of the techniques are directly drawn from the exemplars. However, NLP spawns new techniques *without* exemplars because it has a theoretical basis that allows that. Here is a big statement for you to ponder:

NLP is nothing if not the sum of its parts. Isn't that something? Now let us show you how we see this as a stack. It goes from the most *superficial*, at the top, to the most *abstract* and *profound*, at the bottom:

- **Techniques** (e.g. phobia cure)
- **Technical Perspectives** (e.g. sense modalities)
- **Purposes** (e.g. excellence in coaching)
- **Philosophy** (e.g. presuppositions)
- **Spirit of Innovation and Integration** (e.g. trans-theoretical thinking)
- **Moral Imperatives** (e.g. good of humanity, healing)

Why Isn't NLP a Mainstream Approach?

There you have it. This is one of the most difficult, if not THE most disturbing, questions to answer. As active practitioners in the field, we get this question quite a lot. Mostly, from other NLP advocates! Rarely a client would come in and ask such questions. Since you bought this book and kept reading beyond the first few pages, here is an answer that should / could / would (we hope) ease your mind.

Here is a known fact: Neuro Linguistic Programming has had a *significant influence* on psychotherapy, counseling, sales, coaching, leadership, and plenty of other professional fields. Trainers and therapists have borrowed techniques from Neuro Linguistic Programming or been influenced by it. However, Neuro Linguistic Programming has not gained a lasting place in academic work, and few mainstream therapists acknowledge it. There are several primary reasons.

One reason is that it attracted very diverse, and not always competent or honest advocates. We know some of these people, do we not? Another reason is that serious academic research institutes and leaders were not supportive of NLP, for their own reasons.

Unfortunately, researchers focused on the wrong things. They chose aspects that were *easy* to research, but didn't really represent NLP. Also, a fair amount of the initial writings on NLP (excluding The

Structure Of Magic, volume I and II) was mostly for self-help and less-academically-educated readers, and **there was no widely accepted central body to establish standards.** Because the most central fundamental nature of Neuro Linguistic Programming is as a means of modeling and creating training, it was destined to sprout offshoots that were quite diverse.

On top of this, people tend to *confuse* NLP with the techniques that come from it. They get the impression that NLP has no cohesive identity or that it is just a way to promote success seminars or hypnotize people. We had the same conception of this field before studying it thoroughly. We are not going to point fingers and blame anyone for that unfortunate development. Who's fault it is and why it had to come about this way - these are questions for historians, not for therapists. The average self-help seeker jumped on the NLP-training-wagon instantly. This was certainly the same impression that academics got. They looked for clear-cut ideas, but found in NLP a *mish-mash* of unscientific thinking that obscured the essence and contributions of NLP. For them, there was no "*there*" there.

The result is that many therapists use techniques that have sprouted from NLP, but without knowing (or acknowledging) where it came from.

This has left NLP to be identified with the more outlandish or marginalized practitioners, or simply disregarded or forgotten. Much of the writing of NLP practitioners also detracted from its credibility because it had a scattered or pedantic style. It appears that NLP's emphasis on innovation, "bite-sized" techniques, and grandiose promises tended to attract people with unaddressed symptoms of attention deficit disorder (ADD/ADHD) or other problems in need of insight. This seems to have produced a self-perpetuating cycle that sealed the fate of NLP in so far as the mainstream is concerned.

This meant that the greatest assets left to promote NLP were the *clients* of the NLP practitioners. Their voices, though largely positive, were not collectively strong enough to propel NLP into a status as lasting as cognitive psychotherapy, but NLP did have a strong wave of interest that lasted roughly twenty years. Ok, we are not here to cry over the past or protest or smash any researcher's door (or window). We are here to learn how to help our clients better and "do NLP" the right way. Perhaps, as time goes by and more clients reach their outcomes, the mainstream mental health field will acknowledge and recognize the enormous contribution we all had to their own professional growth.

One mission of this book is to bridge the gap between psychotherapy and NLP. I hope you will agree that it provides well-grounded approaches that can be of great practical value to therapists and other consultants in providing rapid help for many issues as well as bolstering longer-term work. We now know that many concepts that found their way into Neuro Linguistic Programming training, some more than four decades ago, were not really supported by adequate observation, experience, or scientific understanding.

Nonetheless, you can still find a lot of those out-dated old-fashioned concepts and methodologies in many NLP programs today.

This is testimony to the power of *traditions, groupthink, and wishful thinking*. In contrast, this book you're holding brings the core assumptions and functions of NLP into the foreground, showing them at work in modern practices. I hope you find that it makes NLP more accessible as it provides fresh techniques and explanations that expand your repertoire in a scientifically defensible way.

What we remind ourselves every day are the words of Richard Bandler, the famous co-founder of Neuro Linguistic Programming: *"NLP is an attitude and a methodology that leaves behind a trail of techniques."* Any attitudes and methodologies are bound to improve and change in time. We truly believe that now is the best time to acknowledge that fact and take a new perspective when studying this field.

Fundamental Assumptions of NLP

The *presuppositions* of Neuro Linguistic Programming, as these assumptions are called, are an excellent starting point for establishing the core of NLP. These presuppositions are the key guidelines for learning and practicing NLP, as well as for your own success.

There is no universally agreed upon set of NLP presuppositions, but the following list is representative of those in existence. They are discussed in detail in The Big Book Of NLP Techniques. Since the presuppositions are so fundamental, I'm including them here in case you'd like to review them. I provide them with a little working over to fit the purposes of this book.

1. The 'map' is not the 'territory'. We base our actions on our mental map of the world. Knowing that the map is not the territory makes you more flexible and adaptable.

2. People repeatedly respond according to their internal maps. Understanding your client's mental map gives you very important tools. Learning that map brings forth your natural curiosity and creativity.

3. Meaning operates context-dependently. If you really want to understand what something means to someone, you have to understand the situation.

4. Mind-and-body affect each other. We don't just think with our brains, we think with our bodies. Science is revealing more about this all the time.

5. Individual skills function by developing and sequencing of rep systems. This relates to the analysis of representational systems.

6. We respect each person's model of the world. You may not agree with everyone, but if you respect their model of the world, you can understand it and find ways to create more understanding, less conflict, and more good outcomes.

7. Person and behavior describe different phenomena. We "are" more than our behavior. The idea that we are more than our behavior is a very profound idea. Most people are on the verge of a very expanded way of being in the world, and don't even know it. We have no idea what any person's true potential or destiny are. This assumption helps to promote an assumption of human potential that transcends archaic moralism that over-defines people.

8. Every behavior has utility and usefulness–in some context. This idea can be very counter-intuitive, but can liberate extraordinary accomplishments. The Ericksonian concept of utilization is a good example to study.

9. We evaluate behavior & change in terms of context and ecology. This stems from the influence

of systems theory on NLP. Systems theory applies to the human body, to families, organizations, ecology, nations, and the world. This presupposition reminds us to consider the systems impact or, as we say, the ecological impact of any change under consideration.

10. We cannot not communicate. Your clothes, your accent, your body language, subtle expressions that flit across your face, all signal things to the people around you. A key benefit of this assumption is that the more you can align your unconscious and conscious motives, the more your subtle behaviors will communicate the right message. One of the biggest ingredients for charisma is this alignment, or coherence.

11. The way we communicate affects perception & reception. You don't just communicate a digital message. You send out your own collection of submodalities that affect how you are perceived, and even others' ability to perceive you accurately. The valuable lessons of NLP on creating rapport are a great contribution stemming from this presupposition.

12. The meaning of communication lies in the response you get. This is one of the most fundamental and early lessons to get from your study of NLP. Regardless of what you intended to say, the communication is what the other person heard.

13. The one who sets the frame for the communication controls the action. Like our brains, communication doesn't exist in a vacuum. You can exert much more influence when you understand the frame around a communication.

14. There is no failure, only feedback. This presupposition inspires you to turn your failures into learning experiences.

15. The person with the most flexibility exercises the most influence in the system. Since you can depend on change, you must depend on your adaptive creativity. NLP stresses the importance of meta-level thinking.

16. Resistance indicates the lack of rapport. If your customer is resisting doing what is best, don't get mad, get rapport.

17. People have the internal resources they need to succeed. This belief generates excellence, because when you believe in people's internal resources, you believe in your clients and your respect your competitors.

18. Humans have the ability to experience one-trial learning. This presupposition encourages us to liberate the insight and creativity needed to live with a meta level view in a truly awake state, and to live with inspiring objectives.

19. All communication should increase choice. When you pay attention to the frame of communication, and when you develop the learning and flexibility that NLP teaches, you become a master communicator. You develop the ability to expand choices. This presuppositions urges you to knock down barriers to choice when you communicate.

20. People make the best choices open to them when they act. Never take for granted that other people know what you know. They may have all the options that you have, but they don't know it. People make bad choices and limit themselves because they have not connected to the inner resources that will liberate them.

21. As response-able persons, we can run our own brain and control our results. This is the most fundamental discovery that people make as they become more effective.

CBDR

Cognitive behavioral deconstruction and repatterning (CBDR) is not a term you will find prior to this book, but we are using it to describe a fundamental feature of NLP and cognitive behavioral therapy (CBT), which is *chunking down* (breaking down into smaller components) of a person's cognitive processes and physiology. For example, if you break down a person's relapse into alcohol abuse into a sequence of smaller elements, you are in a better position to create a relapse prevention plan, such as that advocated by Gorski, a key thinker in substance abuse treatment. You would be able to identify relapse triggers in the environment as well as in your client's thinking and physical states. From there, you would create a different structure. For example, when relapse signs or triggers appear, the client and members of their support system would be instructed to act very differently, doing things such as increasing the number of support meetings and reducing the amount of stress (external, state, and behavioral strategies), or resuming the practice of thoughts that serve as antidotes for addictive thinking (internal cognitive strategies).

Note that psychosocial intervention is exemplified here, as both behavioral (with family or support group involvement of a social nature) and cognitive (the psycho- part) are incorporated into the intervention program. Except for practitioners influenced by NLP or somatic psychology, CBT practitioners have tended to focus too narrowly on thoughts and behavior, but give inadequate attention to reprocessing and state management. We will make sure you understand these two things.

Sensory Modalities or Representational Systems

NLP emphasizes sense modalities in doing CBDR. *CBT* tends to emphasize the digital auditory (self talk). Since the 1960's, however, CBT has had a handle on the importance of irrational, semi-conscious or unconscious thoughts. EMDR has continued with this tradition by reprocessing memories in a way that includes cognitive work with thoughts that may have not previously been consciously articulated.

Reprocessing

Although NLP has not made use of this term, reprocessing is very important in NLP. In fact, a key goal of this book is to bring out just how important it is, because many NLP practitioners do not realize how much they rely on it. Once you understand it, you will see opportunities to enhance your use of this powerful aspect of therapy. Techniques that use it have tended to treat it as if they have discovered it, refraining from using a generic term. A source of misunderstanding about it is that is cognitive therapy, reprocessing has focused exclusively on making thought patterns more realistic and productive, ignoring the important somatic aspect. The *somatics* of reprocessing are that we are physically "designed" to digest our experiences, making them into useful information.

Many behavioral, emotional, mental, and developmental problems come from a failure to reprocess traumatic or overwhelming experiences. By modeling various practices that do the deeper form of reprocessing, a model has emerged that can be taught without locking the practitioner into a particular practice.

One of these practices is EMDR. *EMDR* involves more than reprocessing and is a very well-developed approach. Thus, it would be misleading to caution the reader against being "locked" into EMDR. We only mean that, with a generic understanding of reprocessing, you will see it wherever it takes place, rather than only when you look through the lens of a particular practice. This will create many therapeutic opportunities for you as well as making you more intuitive when applying techniques that have reprocessing as an active ingredient.

Strategies

By viewing a sequence of successful (or unsuccessful) behaviors as a *strategy*, NLP is expressing the assumptions that make it a powerful source of success and change. NLP did not invent this perspective, but it is central to NLP. We believe that NLP has done a lot to propagate this perspective in mainstream psychotherapy.

NLP practitioners have shown endless creativity in analyzing strategies. By using colorful, compelling, and metaphorical methods, these practitioners have made NLP more accessible to their clients. These methods have included *parts work* (subpersonalities), *spatial placement* (putting parts in various locations on the floor), *time-line* work (creating an imaginary timeline).

From deconstruction, it becomes possible to "re-assemble" and create new strategies for success. For the purposes of this book, we will call these methods "repatterning." Again, with colorful and accessible methods, clients are drawn into life-changing work. Techniques such as *parts negotiation, mapping across*, and *collapsing anchors*, are combined with methods such as *future pacing* to achieve this. NLP has generally been conceived as very time-limited techniques that are not necessarily integrated into a longer arc of work on multiple interrelated problems. But the NLP practitioner that uses NLP presuppositions and skills to integrate modern psychotherapy and neurobiological knowledge will find themselves with endless opportunities to expand the problems that they can work with. An important aspect of this is to use longer-term strategic thinking, seeing the course of treatment as a longer arc of strategy and integration that we call *matrixing*.

Modern Ethics

Yes, this section is worth reading. Most people, including NLP practitioners, feel that we are ethical people. But it's one thing to be successful and have your heart in the right place, and it's another to have the understanding of ethics that you need in order to take on challenging cases—or even not-so-challenging cases. Here's why:

1. Too many well-meaning people are getting into trouble. Most of us have a few ethical blind spots—areas that we just haven't thought about. Yet these blind spots can have serious consequences if we happen to run into a problem.

2) Innocent misunderstandings about ethics and related laws may result in serious legal consequences.

3) Coaches must be knowledgeable about the law and ethics. There are laws and regulations that apply to coaches (or that can apply, depending on the circumstances) that you may not know about. Generally, coaching and NLP training give ethics little, if any, attention. However, coaches do sometimes come under the authority of mental health licensing boards when they get into trouble. You should know how to avoid this.

4) Even though you try to screen out clients that are not appropriate for your practice, it is inevitable that

you will occasionally find yourself working with someone who has some serious issues that you are not prepared to work with. You need to have policies and procedures for evaluating, screening, referring, and transferring these people. A lot of coaches do this by the seat of their pants. Sometimes, this causes problems for them.

5) It is possible that we will cause significant problems for clients if we are unsure about one or two key ethical points.A bad result can cause the client to shy away from getting the help that they need in the future, or worse.

6) So much thought has been put into ethics and how to explain laws to therapists and others that they may apply to, that it would be crazy not to dip into this information on a regular basis in order to be informed, stay up-to-date, and have the proper policies in place.

A little history: Laws, regulations, and ethical guidelines have been evolving for a long time, and they are continuing to undergo changes. Laws and ethics pertaining to therapy are dramatically different from those of forty years ago. Generally speaking, we're talking about vast improvements, not a mindless intrusion of bureaucracy.

Did you know that ethical standards for healers date back to the Hippocratic Oath, developed roughly 2,500 years ago, and even farther back to the Nigerian healer's code? As you can imagine, much of the impetus for regulating professionals has come from problems with the professionals' conduct. Enforcement actions range from letters of warning or other sanctions to punishments, not to mention civil liability that can result in lawsuits. Speaking of licensing boards: Coaches are not regulated as psychotherapists by licensing boards. But if a board comes to feel that a coach is practicing psychotherapy, there may be a problem. Although boards, at least in the U.S., are not actively looking for coaches that might be crossing that line, there are ways that coaches can come to the attention of licensing boards. This happens when a dissatisfied client files a grievance with such a board. Clients are especially likely to file a grievance with the state licensing board when there is a conflict over money, disappointment with services, or the client feels they have been used in some way, such as through a sexual relationship. When a coach or therapist tries to pull out of a sexual relationship with an ex-client, the ex-client may become quite vindictive.

One way clients can be disappointed is if you charge an unusually high fee and create unusually high expectations. Another way is if you create expectations that you are like a psychotherapist and then miss key moves that a therapist might make. The coaches that are the most vulnerable to making a mistake like this are the ones that began creating a defensive style during their childhood in which they tended to cultivate a fantasy of elevated competence in order to protect against feeling socially marginalized and inadequate. That comment sounds pretty harsh, but it is about a common occurrence.

Take care not to give the impression that you are providing psychotherapy or treatment for mental disorders.

Coaches can come under the purview of licensing boards if the board thinks that your promotional materials or actions put you in the position of providing a service that they license. If you look at the legal definition of psychotherapy in your state or other authority, you will see how this could happen. In some states, the definition of psychotherapy is vague. A key concern is that the coach will end up with a person whose hidden mental health issues can cause problems for the coach, if not an outright bad outcome for the client. Coaches should become familiar with signs of mental and emotional issues that may lead to problems, specifically because these coaches (by the scope of their professional responsibility) are not performing mental health assessments and clients may not disclose mental health issues, even if they are aware of them.

Ask about previous mental health problems and treatment, and determine whether there are outstanding issues that may not have been adequately treated. All coaches should be prepared to refer to trusted mental health professionals. Besides, networking with mental health workers may yield clients for your coach's services. Therapists should refer people seeking success coaching to someone like you, unless this is one of their specialties already. Licensed clinicians have their blind spots, as research into the art and science of diagnosis tells us. Many therapists tend to have a pet diagnosis that they use more than the average therapist.

Very common areas where therapists fail to appropriately treat or refer are sleep problems, domestic violence, substance abuse, cognitive disabilities, dissociation, and subtle brain injuries. The takeaway message for therapists is: get deep into assessment issues and stay current. While we're at it, stay up on the legal landscape as well. I have provided below my own ethical guidelines. If you review them, you will probably think of various situations where they can have some relevance and wisdom. Although coaching programs tend to provide little or no training in law and ethics, we feel that this deserves your attention. I hope you will absorb and consistently apply these guidelines.

This code of ethics is adapted from models of major organizations representing licensed psychotherapists. However, it is written specifically for coaches and consultants who are not necessarily members of such an organization. It is necessary to understand the following guidelines in order to function in a truly professional manner. This is because these guidelines can help to protect your reputation and safety, help you avoid trouble, help protect the public, and help protect the reputation of NLP coaching and consulting as professions.

These guidelines won't cover every situation you encounter, but they are very well-rounded, representing millions of person-years of professional practice.

Although these guidelines are not intended as legal advice, the codes that they are modeled after have evolved hand-in-hand with the evolution of laws intended to protect the public and ensure the usefulness of the practitioners those laws regulate. Following these guidelines can help you avoid problems such as practicing medicine or psychotherapy without a license or violating the boundaries of clients.

Do not hesitate to contact a lawyer and review relevant laws and liability issues when potential legal issues arise. When there is any doubt, it is always better to call sooner rather than later. Compared to the attitudes of many coaches, these guidelines may seem strict. In fact, where success coaching between peers is involved and mental health issues are not being treated, you may find that the guidelines concerning dual relationships can be relaxed without creating an ethical breach.

However, it is very easy to err in this area, so we recommend additional consultation and training specifically in this area for all coaches. Another good example is name-dropping and client testimonials. In psychotherapy, this is considered unethical. Getting a client to agree to this is considered imposing on a client in a manner that is not in the client's best interest because it means publicly acknowledging a mental health problem.

As you know, mental health problems are subject to a great deal of social stigma and discrimination in areas as serious as employment and health insurance coverage in countries that do not provide national coverage. In coaching for success, a client testimonial might not be of much concern, because there is no admission of having a disability or disorder.

My advice is to always put the welfare of your client first, making sure that any testimonials do not convey any traits that could result in stigma or discrimination.

Code of Ethics for NLP Practitioners and Coaches

I. Basic Responsibilities

NLP practitioners support client welfare and rights, and the ethical and constructive use of their services. When clients are not physically present during sessions, as in phone sessions, NLP practitioners take extra measures to meet their responsibilities to clients as needed.

1. NLP practitioners support **non-discrimination**, and provide equal consideration regardless of race, gender, religion, national origin, age, sexual orientation, disability, socioeconomic, or marital status. NLP practitioners take reasonable measures to accommodate clients with physical disabilities.

2. NLP practitioners understand that their clients trust them, and so they **refrain from exploiting** that trust. They also understand that dual relationships can become more complicated than expected and result in bad outcomes or the perception of an ethical breach. NLP practitioners **avoid creating any relationships with their clients that are at all likely to impair their judgment** or tempt them to exploit the client. This is especially important where there are ongoing sessions, as opposed to one or a few sessions that are not highly personal.

3. It is questionable to have a **"dual relationship,"** meaning one in which the practitioner and client engage in a different relationship at the same time, such as by also being business partners. Before considering an

additional relationship, the practitioner should allow a reasonable amount of time to elapse after the sessions are complete.

When you cannot avoid a dual relationship, as may occur in a small town, the practitioner will take precautions and create limits for that relationship to ensure that they maintain good judgment and refrain from any exploitation. In any case, sex and dating are inadvisable when in a practitioner-client relationship, and for a reasonable amount of time afterwards.

Where there is significant likelihood of a dual relationship, the practitioner will consider referring the person to another practitioner.

Examples of dual relationship actions include borrowing money, hiring, engaging in a business venture with, or engaging in a close personal relationship with a client. This may also apply to the client's spouse, partner or family members.

4. NLP practitioners honor their **professional commitment** to clients. This includes refraining from abandoning or neglecting clients whose sessions are not complete. To this end, NLP practitioners maintain procedures to support this, such as providing contact information and instructions as to what to do in case of an emergency or in case the NLP practitioner is away, and by terminating sessions properly. This should include a professional will with instructions as to how to transfer, maintain or properly dispose of any confidential or important records.

5. NLP practitioners **stop seeing clients for appropriate reasons only**, and do so in an ethical

manner. These reasons may include the client not benefiting adequately, there is not a good reason to continue, the NLP practitioner is experiencing some kind of impairment such as mental illness, or the relationship has developed a significant ethical problem. for clinically sound reasons and in an appropriate manner. When ending sessions, the NLP practitioner makes sure that any referrals for services or other arrangements are made promptly.

6. NLP practitioners **do not continue sessions with clients purely for their own financial gain**, but it is ethical to discontinue when fees are not paid.

7. NLP practitioners **are not gurus, and are not adamant about any advice they offer** except where safety and emergencies are concerned. NLP practitioners respect the right of their clients to make their own decisions in all areas of their lives, including personal relationships. At the same time, the practitioner will help clients understand the consequences of their decisions, and will give them enough information that clients can make informed decisions about NLP. This information includes the potential risks and benefits of NLP based on the client's situation and capacities.

8. NLP practitioners **inform clients all key policies in advance**. These include the extent of their availability for emergencies and for other contacts between sessions, as well as issues such as fees, no show charges and other fee-related policies. These include whether extended sessions cost more, and how the client will be

enabled to decide on whether to accept an extended session.

9. NLP practitioners **obtain written consent before making any kind of media recording** of sessions. The consent will include the conditions in which the recording can be played and who will experience it.

10. NLP practitioners will explain to their client that the content of their sessions will be kept **confidential**, and the practitioner will honor this into perpetuity. In the event of a court order or safety issue, the practitioner is not required to maintain confidentiality. The client should understand this in advance.

11. NLP practitioners inform clients of their **qualifications and experience** prior to providing services. This can be in the form of a written summary.

12. If there are to be **electronic communications**, NLP practitioners inform their clients of the potential risks to confidentiality, what to do if there is no response (there may have been a technical problem) and how emergencies communicated electronically will be handled.

13. **If the client sees another practitioner** of some kind, such as a mental health provider, the NLP practitioner will provide all useful information when requested by the client. The practitioner will not withhold this information because fees have not been paid. The NLP practitioner will collaborate with practitioners as needed for the welfare of the client, when given permission by the client.

II. Scope of Practice and Referrals

NLP practitioners do not work with clients who have problems that the practitioner does not have **qualifications and skills** to work with, and they **refer** to appropriate professionals as needed.

1. The NLP practitioner will **refer clients** to appropriate medical or psychotherapy treatment providers when there is a concern that **assessment or treatment of symptoms of medical or mental disorders may be needed**.

2. The NLP practitioner is as **aware of the limits of his or her skills** as they are of their abilities. This is called **scope of practice**. As a result, the practitioner **prevents harm by knowing when and how to refer** clients for treatment of possible medical or psychological disorders.

3. The NLP practitioner **learns to recognize symptoms** that may indicate medical and psychological disorders so that they will be effective and timely in making referrals.

III. Confidentiality

NLP practitioners take their clients' privacy seriously. They understand that clients may divulge personal information that they would not want shared with anyone else. Personal information can harm peoples' careers, relationships, and other important life areas. Except for urgent safety concerns, NLP practitioners do not make moral decisions that would lead them to violate the privacy of their clients, and they never indulge in gossip. Practitioners have unique confidentiality responsibilities because the "patient" in a therapeutic relationship may be more than one person. The overriding principle is that NLP practitioners respect the confidences of their patient(s).

1. NLP practitioners are best known for providing coaching that enhances success and well being, and do not treat mental illnesses, therefore, so long as no coercion is involved, the practitioner may solicit permission to use client's recommendations and names in communications and advertising, and in teaching or presenting. **The client must clearly understand the potential consequences and nature of the use of their name, and give permission in advance and in writing** on a form that includes this information. This can prevent serious misunderstandings later. **The NLP practitioner avoids this practice if there is any doubt about the client's objectivity**, such as occurs if the client feels dependent upon the NLP practitioner or confers authority to the NLP practitioner in some manner.

2. NLP practitioners **maintain the total privacy of their clients**, including their names or any information that could identify them. **The only exceptions** to this are a) any legal requirements, such as a court order, b) the need to use specific information to defend themselves in a court action (and the release of information is limited to what is necessary only), c) as needed in order to pursue fees in a legal action (and this is limited to the name of the client, the dates of the sessions, the amount owed, a signed form showing that the client has agreed to fees or policies but that does

not contain information about the client's problems, and the service provided, d) as permitted by the client.

3. NLP practitioners **maintain client records in a safe and secure manner**. They are aware of the risks and limitations of any technology used, and take appropriate steps to prevent breaches. They take extra cautions when transmitting or receiving client information. They dispose of records, including any hardware containing them, such as computer memory devices, in a manner that fully protects confidentiality.

4. NLP practitioners ensure that their **employees, contractors or other personnel maintain confidentiality**, and that they only have access to information that is necessary for the conduct of business and in a manner that the client understands and accepts.

IV. Professional Competence and Integrity

NLP practitioners **maintain high standards** of professional competence and integrity.

1. NLP practitioners **maintain records** of their sessions as needed for competent practice, for maintenance of any signed agreements, for reference in case there is a time lag between sessions, for consulting with other helping professionals, billing, and for any other purposes as needed.

2. NLP practitioners **seek professional assistance as needed** for any problems that may interfere with their performance or judgment.

3. NLP practitioners as teachers or presenters, **present accurate information** from reputable sources.

4. NLP practitioners develop the understanding necessary to work with **people of other cultures**. The identify the cultural and ethnic background and related needs of their clients so that they may provide effective services.

5. NLP practitioners **stay up-to-date in their field** through ongoing educational experiences. They also get ongoing continuing education that expands their knowledge pertaining to psychology and health, because of the diverse issues that clients bring.

6. NLP practitioners **maintain a reputation for honesty, fairness and ethics** in their lives. They refrain from any kind of harassment, exploitation or illegal activity.

7. NLP practitioners **do not provide any services that are outside of their abilities and legal scope** of practice. Unless qualified and legally sanctioned, NLP practitioners do not treat or offer to treat mental or physical illnesses. While people may improve in these areas as a result of NLP, the practitioner does not promote his or her services as a form of treatment. Promoted services may include training on NLP, including self-NLP, stress management, coaching, and stress management, (barring any legal or ethical concerns).

8. NLP practitioners make sure that **any new types of clients they see or skills they use are appropriate from a legal and ethical point of view**, and will be performed competently as a

result of having the proper training, supervision, consultation or experience as needed.

9. NLP practitioners **do not provide services that will conflict with a person's psychotherapy**. The practitioner uses special caution and consideration with a potential client who is receiving psychotherapy. This is because the person may have a mental disorder that places special needs upon any relationship that may result in focusing on memories or goals, or that may induce emotional awareness or deep relaxation. Generally, the practitioner is advised to consult with the psychotherapist before starting sessions. It may be appropriate to proceed when the client is fully able to indicate that they are stable and can tolerate the activities listed in this section, such as experiencing increased awareness.

10. NLP practitioners take reasonable steps to **prevent the distortion or misuse of their approach** and knowledge, particularly by the media and influential persons. This includes steps such as letters to the editor, personal communications, and collective communication from practitioners.

11. NLP practitioners want to **affect people and their community in the most positive way possible**, and they want to generate and preserve respect for their approach, so they **exercise care in their public statements**, live or in any medium. As part of their ongoing education, NLP practitioners learn how to recognize and engage in rational and ethical rhetoric, debate and public

discourse. This includes understanding and avoiding logical fallacies.

12. NLP practitioners **only engage in research when they have adequate support, skills and knowledge** to do so. NLP practitioners do not make public statements as to the results of their research unless they are adequately trained and competent to carry out reliable research. NLP practitioners gain the knowledge pertaining to research, and will only talk about the results of others' research when they can do so competently and credibly.

V. Responsibility to Students

As with clients, NLP practitioners **do not exploit the trust** of their students.

1. NLP practitioners apply the **ethical guidelines in their conduct with students** as with clients. This refers to exploitation, dual relationships that may impair judgment, sexual contact, and sexual harassment.

2. NLP practitioners take reasonable measures to **prevent their students from holding themselves out as able to perform services and skills that are beyond their actual skills and experience**. This is reflected in the standards and testing related to any certifications or references provided.

4.3 NLP practitioners who act as teachers or who supervise students that are gaining experience **maintain and enhance their teaching or supervision skills, and get consultation** as needed.

VI. Responsibility to Colleagues and Other Professionals

NLP practitioners **treat colleagues and other professionals with courtesy, respect and fairness**. They cooperate with their colleagues in order to support the well being of their clients and community.

1. NLP practitioners **respect their colleagues privacy**, and maintain any confidences that their colleagues share with them, except where a clear ethical or legal need requires disclosure.

2. NLP practitioners make reasonable efforts to **help colleagues who are impaired** by problems such as substance abuse or mental illness.

VII. Responsibility to NLP

NLP practitioners work to **advance the goals of NLP and respect for the professionals involved** in NLP.

1. NLP practitioners continue to act in accordance with the ethics of their profession, **without being compromised by their employment or membership** in an organization.

2. NLP practitioners **give credit** to people who contribute to their publications in proportion to the contribution and according to traditional publication practices. This includes giving attribution to the people who came up with original ideas and contributions.

3. NLP practitioners **take responsibility for the marketing and promotion** of their work, training

offerings, and publications, ensuring that it is done accurately and honestly.

4. NLP practitioners recognize the importance of **contributing to a better community and society**. They engage in practices that support this, such as devoting a portion of their professional activity to services for which there is little or no financial return.

5. NLP practitioners recognize the importance of **supporting laws and regulations that pertain to NLP and that serve the public interest**, and of fighting or altering laws and regulations that do not.

VIII. Responsibility to the Legal System

NLP practitioners recognize and understand their r**ole in the legal system** and their duty to remain objective and honest.

1. NLP practitioners who have questions or concerns about a case or practice that may have legal repercussions consult a qualified attorney in order to ensure that their conduct is in compliance with the law. They never assume that they know the law through using common sense, their impression of what is fair, or information that is not from a legal authority or that they do not fully understand.

2. NLP practitioners who give testimony in legal proceedings **testify truthfully** and avoid making misleading statements.

3. NLP practitioners **understand laws that have a bearing** upon their practices, directly or indirectly, and comply with those laws.

4. NLP practitioners **do not publicly express professional opinions about an individual's mental or emotional condition**, unless they clearly state the limitations of their knowledge of the situation and that they are offering a personal opinion. This is to help ensure legally appropriate testimony, and to avoid making statements that may legally compromise the practitioner or other people.

IX. Financial Arrangements

NLP practitioners make **financial arrangements** with clients and students that are understandable, and conform to accepted professional practices and legal requirements.

1. NLP practitioners **do not offer or accept payment for referrals**. This prevents a loss of objectivity in making referrals that could exploit and bring harm to clients or divert them from a more appropriate referral.

2. NLP practitioners **do not financially exploit** their clients.

3. NLP practitioners **disclose in advance** their fees and how they will be computed. They make sure their clients understand matters such as charges for canceled or missed appointments and any interest to be charged on unpaid balances, at the beginning of treatment. They **give reasonable notice** of any changes in these policies or amounts.

4. NLP practitioners give **reasonable notice** to clients with unpaid balances of their intent to sue, or to refer for collection. Whenever legal action is taken, therapists will **avoid disclosure of clients' personal information** such as their problems. If the practitioner refers to a collection agency, they avoid disclosure of clinical information and select an ethical agency.

5. NLP practitioners **normally don't accept non-monetary remuneration** such as goods or services for their services. This is because it can create conflicts of interest and lead the client to feel exploited. This can harm the therapist-client relationship.

X. Advertising

NLP practitioners enable potential clients to **make informed choices** regarding their services.

1. NLP practitioners are **honest about the current nature** of their skills, training and experience.

2. NLP practitioners **advertise honestly**.

3. NLP practitioners display their name, credentials and business name in a way that **does not mislead** potential clients in any way or create any unjustified expectation.

4. NLP practitioners **correct, wherever possible, false, misleading, or inaccurate information** about their qualifications, services, or products.

5. NLP practitioners **use great care in using any testimonials** in a manner that is in compliance with their existing agreement with the client or ex-

client, and refrain from soliciting or using testimonials in any way that interferes with the best interests of that person.

6. NLP practitioners don't use NLP or other initials after their names to give the impression of a license or academic degree that they do not have.

The Relationship as the Active Ingredient

When researchers review all of the best research in psychotherapy, they are conducting a form of research called *meta* research. Fairly early in this exploration, it emerged that the technique being used didn't matter much, if at all. Instead, the quality of the relationship was the factor that was most pronounced.

Currently, some specific techniques are emerging as being important to certain problems. This is partly because of progress in therapy, and partly because research is becoming more sophisticated and focused with more specific questions. If this give the impression that NLP is not important, we think there is something that the research is overlooking.

NLP is so focused on distilling out the most important ingredients to change, that we suspect that if researchers could focus on the best NLP practitioners, and target the problems that NLP is best suited to, it would inform research on psychotherapy. Fortunately, as we will soon explain, research is actually moving in a similar direction. But let's consider this business about the relationship for a moment. An interesting thing about this is that if the client feels that the therapy is likely to be effective within the first two or three sessions, and then the therapy is likely to produce good results. This speaks to the perceptiveness of the clients as well as their capacity to utilize the therapy. What causes what? If we say that the relationship is what is making the therapy effective, we might have the arrow of causality pointing the wrong way.

What if the quality of the relationship is not the cause of good therapy? What if it is a sign of the capacities within the client and therapist that produce good results? That would be no surprise. We know that clients who are more intelligent are more likely to benefit from therapy. But intelligence as conceived by these researchers is just one aspect of the strengths that put a person in a good position to make the best use of therapy. And it's a two way street.

The better the *capacity* of the therapist (intelligence, emotional capacity, insight, etc.) the more *useful* the therapist is likely to be to the client, particularly for problems that do not respond well to a cookbook approach. We think that a very important take away message from this research is that the building of capacity in yourself and in your clients is a very important active ingredient for good therapy. This book will help you think about NLP in terms of building such capacities in clients and in yourself.

Emerging Knowledge

Of the specific therapies that are emerging as important for specific problems, we are learning that reprocessing and formal psychoeducation are two important trends. We will have a major focus on reprocessing in this book. *Psychoeducation* is proving to be very important for problems that have been very difficult to treat with previous forms of psychotherapy. Psychoeducation for severe problems may involve something more like a classroom experience, at least at first, than what we would usually think of as psychotherapy. A good example of this is *dialectical behavior therapy*, an approach that is proving to be very valuable for borderline personality disorder. A similar approach that supports the rehabilitation philosophy is proving of great value for severe mental illnesses such as schizophrenia. Material from Mary Ellen Copeland is very enlightening in this regard. Although we won't be going into psychoeducation, we do want to encourage you not to underestimate the value of conscious information for your clients. The more you know about how people cope successfully with issues, the more you will have to offer your clients. Sometimes we can become so occupied with working unconsciously, that we may forget how valuable the conscious mind can be.

Well Being Affecting Attitude

Important discoveries are increasingly uniting our concepts of mind and body. Let's start with the impact of health on attitude. Here is an example: People suffering from *Lyme* disease are considered to have a much higher incidence of mental disorders, including anxiety and depression marked by catastrophic and negative thinking. They also are more likely to have *fibromyalgia*. Disordered sleep harms health and mental functioning. Lyme disease and fibromyalgia sufferers have significant sleep problems. As tempting as it is for zealous advocates of *positive thinking* to blame health and mood problems on negative thinking, it is becoming increasingly clear that there are specific, biological pathways that can disrupt mood and thinking, and that these have nothing to do with bad thinking habits or poor role models. It's quite the opposite.

Although positive thinking is a great asset, a lot of the classic beliefs about positive thinking are symptomatic of primitive defenses and pre-scientific thinking. Here's an example of primitive defenses in action: People are more likely to blame other people for being in bad circumstances, but when it comes to themselves, they are more likely to blame their bad circumstances for causing their problems. Here's another:

The average driver believes that they are *above* average. And another: Of people who are ninety percent sure of something, **forty percent** are wrong. Science is not supporting the belief that positive thinking metaphysically influences our circumstances, or that it dramatically affects our health. A better theory is that people with good attitudes are more *likely* to overcome health problems not because of their attitudes, but because of better health and social standing that contributes to their good attitudes. Excellent support for this attitude comes from our understanding of *post-traumatic stress disorder* (PTSD). In the absence of sufficient biological knowledge, people have come up with explanations for PTSD that are being eclipsed by our growing scientific knowledge. These explanations range from *karma*, to *spirits* from a volcano that exploded four quadrillion years ago, to *psychological defenses* and *spiritual decisions* made about life after experiencing a traumatic incident. If any of these were complete explanations, then PTSD sufferers would not have such dramatic improvements in their functioning after restoration of their sleep or after processing traumatic memories with approaches that have little to do with exorcising negative thoughts or ancient spirits. Counter-intuitively, it may be that therapies that specifically target dysfunctional thinking, generally referred to as *cognitive therapies*, can attribute much of their success to the secondary effects of physical improvements (such as the restoration of sleep) that occur with the support of a caring therapist and the reduction of immediate anxiety through reprocessing (which we will discuss in detail later). In other words, the improvements in thinking may by symptomatic of a *bio-psychological* cascade that leads to deeper physical improvements that resolve PTSD symptoms. This kind of information tells us that we must stay current on our professional research and thinking. No approach is so timeless or profound that it deserves to be insulated from the ongoing progress of science and clinical experience. There's a great word for over-valuing an idea or institution: *mystification*. It means that, by shrouding something in a *mystical aura*, we insulate it from criticism and progress. This has been done with capitalism, socialism, religions, and approaches to therapy and coaching. The result is that the methods become increasingly outdated. Harm results. Eventually, society intrudes. The history of lawsuits against psychotherapists provides some examples of this. Certainly, certain Catholic diocese thought they were *above* the law regarding child abuse. Then some of them were financially destroyed by lawsuits.

First, Avoid Harm

This is not an academic matter. It is a matter of ethics and safety. For example, a number of children have been literally *killed* by *rebirthing* therapists only because these therapists did not understand that their physical interventions with these children had *medical* implications. In other words, the therapists were operating outside of their scope of practice by using physical interventions that they did not really understand. These interventions, involving confining the child in a rolled blanket, resulted in asphyxiation through excessive CO_2 that prevented the children from being resuscitated. Had these therapists not fallen under the spell of *mystification*, they would have recognized the scope-of-practice and safety issues. They would have also learned that child development is much more complicated than the simple-minded and nearly superstitious theories of rebirthing. Cathartic emotional release from birth trauma is not a cure for profound personality problems in children.

This is a drastic example of the harm that can come from substituting a single, convenient "villain" (birth trauma) for the more complicated picture that emerges in legitimate clinical thinking. Have you heard about the young lady that went through rebirthing therapy and told her mother about it? As she described reliving the birth experience her mother started laughing and said, *"You were a cesarean..."* Be cautious of charlatans, and learn NLP well enough to never be considered one.

From this point, you'll be learning very specific interventions and theoretical points that you can apply in coaching or therapy. The patterns in this next section are good for the beginning of your relationship.

Advanced NLP Techniques

We begin therapy by initiating an effective relationship with a client; one that builds mutual trust and that establishes your competence in the eyes of the client. To achieve this, you need to generate positive states, expectations, and outcomes while building a constructive relationship. A valuable skill you will learn in this section is priming, which is a type of memory. The key to priming is cultivating a state in a particular time frame, regardless of how it is anchored.

Priming often relies on implicit memory, which is an unconscious kind of memory. An interesting example of implicit memory can be found in product placement, in which advertisers pay for the appearance of products in movies and other formats. They spend a lot of money on this, because familiarity with a product primes the person to feel more positive about it when they encounter it, even if they don't consciously remember ever seeing the product.

NLP uses the term "priming" to refer to cultivating or triggering a state. Often, this involves unconscious, implicit memories. We begin to prime a client for a state by setting up the conditions that make it easy for them to go into that state. For example, expressing positive feelings and beliefs about a client's identity and helping them to feel less threatened primes their "secure base." A secure base tends to bring out more cooperative and creative behavior in a person. The research on subliminal stimulation for priming a secure base was a real breakthrough. But then, politicians and con artists have known for a long time that attacking a secure base makes people ready to make certain types of rash decisions that play into their hands. If people do not rush to war quickly enough, reason may set in and ruin the plan. When a client experiences a secure base, a resourceful state, a sense of mastery and other positive states, When they work with you, you are making yourself into a trigger for positive states. This priming means that each time they see you, they will tend to experience resourceful states more easily and quickly. This means that your work will become more effective in that regard over time. This is a subtle and general kind of anchoring. The following techniques will illustrate priming in various ways.

Recognition

Of course, it's important for clients to know that you "*get*" them. But among the most important things for you to get are the most serious binds and traumas that they experienced. When a client mentions something that is profoundly important, such as that, you should draw upon your life experience and flash a sign of recognition that shows your client that it registered and that you are not judging them or becoming defensive in some way. First, you must be on the lookout for these profound *disclosures*.

Many times, a client will mention something without *emotional emphasis*. Still, they are likely to look to see how you respond. If you missed the content, that look should signal you to tune into the profundity of what they just revealed. When you notice a *profound* disclosure, here are some excellent ingredients for your response:

1) **Inhale** while slightly extending your upper back and tilting your head up with your mouth part way open and your eye brows slightly lifted.

2) **Exhale fully**. When half way exhaled, acknowledge this in a way that conveys an, *"oh that..."* quality. For example,

"Ah, attorneys..." or "With years lost, right?" or (slightly shaking head) "It's just scary how many people are going through this now." or my favorite: "Isn't that something?"

You don't want to be dishonest, of course. If you really don't know what the experience is about, convey how important it is to you to know more about what it involves and what impact it has had. Either way, you'll probably need to learn more about what the experience means to your client, as well as how it colors their challenges today.

Curiosity

The last things you want reflected in your body language with a client are *rejection, excessive distance* or the quality of *pushing* something *onto* the client. Perhaps the greatest antidote to such tendencies is showing an inquisitive nature.

Curiosity about what the client is saying on all levels draws the client out, especially when it is a calm, grounded curiosity. What follows are the ingredients for creating such an experience.

Ingredients and Typical Evolution

1) **Questions that have no odd quality to them.** They are, at least on the surface, common sense. Remember, this is early in your connection with the client.

2) **Showing your interest and balanced curiosity with body language,** such as leaning forward a bit when the client says something that has an emotional connection or deeper meaning. This shows that you are responsive, and it can feed the client's self-disclosing behavior because attention is a strong reinforcer of behavior.

3) **Questions about the underlying significance.** They can start with a half-baked assumption that morphs into a question. For example, *"I can imagine that when she said that, you could really..."* (making a small sweeping gesture toward your stomach-gestures should show restraint so there is no sense of acting or being an erratic person),"... *well, I mean, what other options could have gone through your mind at that point?"*

Ending the question with an open face shows a hint of appreciation of the client's pain and feeling boxed in.

The client's answer gives the practitioner a sense of the client's level of flexibility and insight. If the client has no sense of having options (as in *"she made me feel that way or do that,"* then the therapist has pulled this out in a context in which there is no sense of impending judgment or "*psychoanalyzing*" the person. Notice that the half-baked assumption is actually a way of establishing an expectation that the client must have feelings about it and connects the client with feelings to some degree, *priming* the client for a deeper answer than you would get with the "talking heads" effect that removes humanity from coaching.

This is very important for eliciting in your own self a healing state. Any time that you begin to feel yourself pushing into the client, distancing too much, or becoming judgmental, this experience is one of the fastest and most useful ways to keep yourself from contaminating the process. It is much easier to think creatively and flexibly when you are in an inquisitive state.

Significance

Nearly everyone wants to be a hero, but people who are *marginalized* want it more. Why else would comic books have a hero who can't reveal his or her identity but is intensely tempted to do so in order to impress someone? You can use this experience with anyone, but *loners*, *underachievers,* or people who are *feeling unappreciated* especially need this in order to trust you. For them, it's a key nutrient as well. In this experience, you will show your connection with their sacrifices and positive intent.

Listen and observe:

1) **What is stressing your client?**

The obvious stressors are external, but you are deeply listening to how the client has internalized real or imagined judgment from *others*, an *authority figure*, or "*society*."

2) **Where is your client's drive and effort coming from?**

Notice what the client is doing to deal with the situation, even if it is destructive or too passive. Ferret out what values are driving the client and which of those are the most intensely felt. The woman recovering from drug abuse and trying to regain custody of her children may not appear to be doing what she is supposed to do, but she probably feels inside that she is working very hard and that her hard work is not being appreciated. This could even be true.

> Recovery from addiction can exhaust others' patience, and this is a painful situation for someone desperate to rejoin society.

You might find that she is terrified of what may happen to her children because of negative stories and news about foster care. You can recognize this as coming from her love for her children and as being protective.

3) **Notice how well, or poorly, your client consciously connects their higher values with their efforts.**

Do they feel that they are driven by high values, or are they perseverating so much about the unfairness or threats in the situation that they experience little inspiration? You can often predict that this is what you'll find because they exude an oppressive fatigue and weariness.

4) **Notice how well they are able to see their efforts as expressing their desire to meet an important challenge.**

Again, the undesirable alternative is the over-focus on threat and unfairness, with the resulting sense of fatigue and wear. If you find yourself becoming irritated at a client's immature lock-on to unfairness and threats, remember that they have been living this, and they have probably experienced a nasty blend of double binds and emotional shocks, if not outright trauma, that has wound them into a tight coil of perseveration. They may also have cognitive difficulties from injuries, mental illness, or addiction. Although it may be appealing to wave your magic wand and produce instant NLP magic, never resent a client for posing a challenge that threatens your ego. Sometimes, cognitive impairment or being locked into a struggle can seem like they are not cooperating or even sabotaging the work. The intrusion of the coach or therapist's ego into the process can be sneaky. Even a hint of this can create a vicious cycle in which the practitioner and client feed into a negative relational dynamic.

You can bounce out of this judgmental state by thinking of the client as a possible candidate for longer-term cognitive rehabilitation, which is something that practitioners can contribute to a great deal. This is because restoring thinking occurs by preparing for and dealing with actual situations and people rather than means, such as cognitive computer games. You can trigger more respect in yourself for the client by engaging them at this level. To complete the experience, you repeatedly link the following things:

1) The client's higher values as fuel for their efforts.

To do this, you show a real appreciation for how hard they are working and struggling. It is important not to be maudlin here, because there must be no exaggerating or acting. A restrained and objective comment will have a stronger impact than a more intense presentation. Then, state that you can see how the client would do this in order to pursue the higher values that you have recognized. You can also link this to something you want to see happen that you feel the client is very likely to agree with. For example, you could say: "There are few things as difficult as recovering from addiction... especially when you have lost so much. Not to mention dealing with all the add-on demands like all these appointments and the harsh timeline. You're under a spotlight that can really distract people and make them feel demoralized. Your love for your children must be incredibly powerful for you to be so totally driven. We really need to work on some stress management skills so you can stay in shape... and make it obvious to the social worker and the judge what you're really about here. Just as an expert runner must avoid getting sick from being too thirsty... we need to make sure you're in good shape for all this. "

Make this a theme, especially in the first phase of your work. **Look for every opportunity to produce this experience.**This will contribute to your motivation as well as your client's, and it will help to keep key goals meaningful and in focus.

Contribution

What if your client could do no wrong?

Taking this position isn't always a good idea, but it is a skill worth practicing because it primes your clients to become more cooperative and creative in finding solutions. This experience is like a chess sequence in that it starts with a set up followed by additional moves.

Try using these ingredients during an entire session with clients that you feel may benefit from it. This will be for them, but also for your practice. Each time your client says something that you feel you need to resist, correct, or negatively judge, look for one of the following opportunities:

1) A need that you can connect their statement to;

2) a value that you can connect their statement to;

3) a feeling, positive or negative that you can connect their statement to, or...

4) a positive objective that you can connect their statement to.

Each time you select one of these connections, also think of a second connection that will begin to create momentum in the direction of a good outcome, either in the short or long term. For example, if the client says that his boss is a real jerk, you might connect this to a feeling such as, *"You look bitterly disappointed. I know you don't want anything getting in the way of enjoying your work and really performing."* When you decided to connect the feeling, you thought at least one step ahead, and saw that bringing the feeling into the foreground would not only show that you can acknowledge his body language and stay relevant, but you also planned to connect the feelings to his values and dreams.

The client thought he was simply angry, but the words "*bitterly disappointed*" not only more accurately reflected his body language, but they also primed him to connect with what he was disappointed about. You may not have known exactly what, but it was most likely something like his career goals, his hopes for his role and contributions in the company, or his desire to function at his best (which is boss was interfering with through emotional stress). By speaking in general or vague terms in the second segment *("...enjoying your work and really performing")* you leave room for him to connect with the specifics on his own terms.

In the rare situation when you are too far off the mark, the client will tell you.

To bring one (or *all*) of these into focus, you might simply ask the client to talk about that. If the client is not good at making such connections right away, you can ask about these things more directly and make the connections for them. *Stumping* the client and having them *squirm* while they try to make connections can simply anchor a state of confusion and helplessness, as well as interfere with the development of rapport. On top of that, it wastes valuable time. And in the rapid therapy field, the more time you waste, the less effective you are (and the least profitable, since you're paid for results, not by the clock).

Memory research has shown that staying with that *"tip of the tongue"* feeling when a memory cannot be verbalized does not strengthen memory power, even if the memory does eventually come into consciousness. Also, it is more important to move the treatment along than it is to give the client practice in articulating things that are not very conscious.

There is nothing wrong with supplying the words for the client, so long as the client feels free to tell you how those words need to be adjusted to more accurately reflect their inner world.

> The more experienced you become, the more consistent you will be in providing just the right words.

This creates a great deal of momentum and efficiency in this kind of interventive experience. Now that you have the client talking about their dreams and needs, you have opened the gate to creating meaningful objectives for your work with them. This is much more productive than "trying" to "get" the client past their anger. That was just the surface emotion anyway. Now look at the kinds of goals that might be on the table, with the client's full interest.

1) Getting into a very creative, positive state when dealing with his boss, and having specific strategies to turn the situation around;

2) Maximizing his confidence and resources to angle for a better position and a better boss;

3) Getting rid of his boss through deft use of office politics and outshining his boss, and...

4) Getting so attuned to his goals and confidence that his boss doesn't shake him and, as a result, is no longer a threat to your client's performance.

5) Or some combination of the above. Your assessment of your client and your client's self knowledge will help you select from goals such as these.

Values Elicitation

There's nothing quite like experiencing heartfelt values. A deep experience of values is inspiring, energizing, and galvanizing. To help a client experience this requires a kind of "deep listening" for the subtext that implies and leads to such values. This version of the experience uses deep experiencing in order to not only prime the client to resourcefully move into experiencing values in this heartfelt manner, but it also makes for a more compelling experience that lends momentum to treatment.

> Once your client makes such connections, you are able to begin connecting their values with actual needs and objectives.

This is a crucial and powerful turning point in treatment. It empowers any number of interventions. For example, clients can learn to communicate in a much more compelling manner when their expression of vision and ideas is infused with heartfelt values. As you interact with your client, construct the best sense of their values as you can. Do not be distracted by the primitive or negative constructs that the client expresses.

Even the most vulgar expression of opinion can yield information about a client's higher values. In addition, their level of consciousness and irrationality can provide vital clues as to how they may be disorganized as a result of specific cognitive impairments, mood disorders, trauma history, impaired early bonding, or even significant signs of mental illness. A middle-aged Jewish couple was able to think like this about a young man who was hounding them with anti-Semitic attacks. They saw that he was desperately trying to gain meaning and self-esteem by aligning himself with something that was larger than him and conferred a kind of power. They discovered that they were able to connect with him and bring out his intense and unfulfilled developmental need for emotional nurturance. They ultimately filled that need by making him a part of their family. This is not to imply that every bigot just needs a little love from the people they are terrorizing, but most people who align with sources of felt authority in a zealous manner have developmental and cognitive issues that can be viewed from a mental health perspective. This story shows that the values you are looking for are connected with needs. If the needs are primitive because of problems such as poor early bonding with parent figures, then the work will almost certainly need to begin at a fundamental level.

Odds are that this will require a psychotherapist with a good deal of patience and an excellent understanding of cognitive and developmental remediation. In any case, once you have your collection of values that are "up" for the client in connection with his or her current issues, you are ready for the next step. But remember that, since values are ultimately universal, you'll have no trouble coming up with values. The objective here is to get a sense of which ones the client is frustrated in expressing and perhaps having difficulty fully connecting with. Help your client *connect* their values with the feelings or behaviors that are at issue. An excellent way is to:

1) Ask them about the outcomes that they would most like to see.

2) Then ask them about the values that the outcomes would support. You can help them find the words and ideas if they are unsure how to express themselves.

For example, a man who was told to see a counselor if he wanted to keep his job was very angry at feeling coerced into treatment. He tended to be too rough with other employees, saying things that sounded too hostile, judgmental, and controlling. The client was able to say that he wanted to be free to express himself in his own way, that some of the employees were stupid, and that he really wanted them to do their best (which included not getting in his way), and that he wanted the business to prosper. With a little help, he connected these things with the following values:

1) Freedom of expression and embracing diversity;

2) Being tough enough to give and take feedback;

3) The realization of human potential;

4) Cooperation for constructive work;

5) Allowing others to do their work without interference; and...

6) Profit.

The counselor now has six "*handles*" with which to bring out more behavior and agreements that are in line with these values.

> Every potential goal can be framed in terms of one or more of these values: Freedom, Composure, Potential, Cooperation, Independence, Profit, __ yours choice___.

For example, with a little help, the client was able to see why his boss would feel it was good for *profit* to send him in for counseling, since the "weaker" employees could not handle the client's demeanor. Also, he could see how the "weaker" employees could function better if he was more "*manipulative*" of them be being a bit more gentle. If you're a parent, isn't it true that your son or daughter would learn more if you "allow" them to fail a certain school assignment, instead of jumping in and doing half (or 99%) of the work for them? Yes, of course you want your 8 years old to get straight A's, but getting the grade is not as important as the process that the child must go through, on their own, to own the competency to get an A.

A side note: one of the most crucial life skills you could ever help a child achieve is to turn failure into feedback. We, as NLP learners, know the importance of such skill. We "know" because we look back (in anger? There's another intervention required here) at our past failures and at our false self-contempt and unfair self-criticism right after, and we do not wish to re-feel like that ever again. So "feedback" is suddenly a good idea. But did you consider installing that desire to learn from failure as if it's the most valuable experience, to your children?

The client was from New York, and had recently been relocated to Denver. The counselor commiserated with him a bit, recognizing that people from the east coast tend to be misunderstood by mid-westerners.

In this context, they were able to agree that making the cultural transition was a meaningful challenge, even if it was inconvenient. It was also kind of like a game, in which you learn to play along with the strange rules of the mid-west, such as not confronting people in a direct, immediate, spontaneous way.

Holding Attention

The next few techniques are intended more for practice than for use exactly as they are presented. This is because these techniques build more impact and control into your speech. You could call that *stylistic intelligence*. The keyword of this section might be *restraint*, because it takes aspects of NLP and applies them in a very narrow-spectrum way to empower your work. I hope you will feel that this is like being able to do fine work with the help of a magnifying glass. I also hope that you find that these systems leverage your existing NLP skills in novel ways that are relevant to your work, at any point of your work. These are very stylistic applications of NLP that you can make your own. At first they may seem very prescriptive, but you'll find that once you practice them, you can make them fit your personality completely as well as to empower it further.

Punctuation

Psychological time is key to attention, frustration, and cooperation in healing practice. You can create a more compelling and time-compressed experience by learning to emphasize (punch up) certain words as you speak. Practice this system while you monitor how intensely people hang on your words as you speak. You may need to desensitize yourself to the experience of people paying intense attention to what you say, and leaving room for you to say it.

You may also find that they want to get in synch and contribute ideas along the same line.

Watch for a slight forward lean or head forward posture, less blinking, and a slightly wide-eyed quality in others as you do this system.

Try out the following versions and listen to recordings of yourself. Be sure to record yourself speaking normally first. These methods are especially helpful when you have a number of things to say, and need to capture attention and make sure that your ideas really register.

The Bi-Lateral

Try this experiment: As you speak, slightly alternate your foot pressure on key words that deserve emphasis. This will alter your state as you speak.

Try saying this sentence, emphasizing the key words marked with an *asterisk** and shifting to the specified left or right foot.

"*For the first** (left) *key word put pressure** (right) *on your left** (left) *foot, and the second** (right) *key word put** (left) *it on your right** (right)."

This may be awkward at first, but it can become automatic with practice. Notice that you can have several words in a row that are not emphasized, but they will not be lost on people. In fact, people can concentrate and digest what you say more easily when you emphasize less key-words.

You may not make a habit of this for presenting, but this practice can change how you experience presenting. In actual presentations, however, you should consider gestures, shifting your weight, and position changes that create bilaterality (side changing) during much of your presentation.

The George Carlin

Entrain your words into consistent beats as you speak. However, don't keep the beat at the same rate. **Speed up and slow down the rate of the rhythm, but keep the words falling on the beat.** You can practice this first by talking while music is playing, and making your words fall on the beat. Once you can do this, let some words fall two to the beat. (In the last sentence *"to the"* would be good for a word pair that double up on a beat. Once you have that, try some *triplets*, where three words cover a single beat. As you practice, you'll notice that it's actually easier and more effective to think in terms of syllables, rather than words. **Try putting this to beats:**

The beats are numbered: "1. SYLlables 2. RAther than 3. BEATS." That's a DA-da-da DA-da-da DA. rhythm. ONE and a TWO and a THREE. This is kind of like, *"Lions and tigers and BEARS, oh my!"*

Two triplets and a whole note.

I call this the *George Carlin* because this was his signature style. His speech was laced with rhythms from the big band era, and this contributed to his hip, cool daddy vibe. Once you have this, then you'll find that as you speak, you can stay on the beat, but also speed and slow the rhythm. Listen to George Carlin's routines, and notice how he speeds and slows while keeping the beat. Bear in mind that many musicians, including Eric Clapton, tap their foot on or just ahead of the beat. This helps them play intense, exciting rhythms that keep the audience engaged. Also, many people report that they have a much easier time learning any new information when there's a rhythm with alternating strong and weak beats. You can read more about the NLP Rhythmic Learning Strategy in The Big Book Of NLP, Expanded.

The Verb Finder

Once you've practiced this, you will not want to use it all the time, but it will inform your word punctuation. (Remember that these are practices that build unconscious skill and discrimination that will enrich your verbal impact and control.) As you SPEAK, only EMPHASIZE the verbs, *except* for the verb "to be." You might be surprised to FIND that is doesn't SOUND as odd as you'd exPECT. Once you get used to this in practice, you will find it is easier to improvise, emphasizing whatever words your intuition tells you to improvise.

The Punctuation Diet

Practicing this can help you pull your emphasis away from words that should not be emphasized. WHEN you EMPHasize the WRONG WORDS, YOU can sound PREACHY and HAVE a SING SONG QUALity to your SPEECH. **Try it this way instead:**

When you EMPHasize the wrong words, you can SOUND preachy and have a SING song quality to your SPEECH.

This style will actually make it seem as though you are taking up less time as you speak. Less *punctuators* creates more contrast, and thus, more interest. The human mind can take in a good number of non-emphasized words, so you will not lose your message by reducing the emphasized words. You actually *collapse psychological time* so that it's easier to listen to you and take in your message. You can use this for pretty much anything you say, whether it is to the media, to clients, negotiating, or in your personal life.

Listen to experts that are very media savvy when they are interviewed. Practice this with things that you typically say. You can mentally rehears, record yourself, and refine the technique to fit your personality.

Movement

These next techniques expand your pacing and leading skills in ways that are sensitive to issues of state management and reprocessing. Each has an introduction that will orient you to its purpose and to what you will be working with. Nuanced Gesturing is a kind of pacing and leading that is much more subtle than the classic description of pacing and leading. It provides some leading simultaneous with initial pacing by contextualizing your client's words with your subtle physical responses to their words and affect.

As a training aid for practitioners, this system can help you become more conscious of your more subtle reactions to your clients so that you can manage your state and body language in subtle ways toward advancing your work as a healer. Your gestures will have the most significance if they are not too restrained or too wild.

Many of your clients will be easily over-stimulated or be highly sensitive about trust and boundaries. You will find that many of your clients respond well to your physical gestures when you employ this system.

You might want to watch a video of yourself to see whether you already do this unconsciously, or whether you do it as well as you think you do already. People gather a tremendous amount of information from people through "non-digital" aspects of communication such as tone of voice and body language.

> By "*flattening*" the "*volume*" of your various non-digital communications, the more subtle elements become more obvious.

Also, by focusing on enhancing your state, you will have more unconscious alignment with your conscious gestures; thus, your communication will be richer and more nuanced. To get used to this approach, practice this system in everyday conversations that are not high stakes. Pay attention to your body language.

Do not attempt to pace your conversation partner. Instead, allow whatever body language you'd care to reveal to be expressed. However, keep your body language somewhat restrained, like water simmering instead of boiling. In order to do this, keep your hand gestures within the frame of your body. Do not allow them to move outside of your silhouette.

Your gestures, whether you are reacting or expressing yourself, should be mostly very small or subtle.

If you are prone to generous gestures or talking with your hands, this may take some practice. Once you get used to this, you will be able to be more selective about when and how you make bigger gestures. This will make them stand out more and have more meaning, because you can produce more contrast in your movement. Also, you will not seem eccentric, if your intensity and quantity of gestures tends to be too high. If you tend to sit very still, you will need to bring your reactions and self-expression out so that you actually have gestures that convey them.

Once you feel comfortable with this, add consciousness of your facial expressions and bodily positioning.

Make subtle shifts in your facial expression, such as a slight and gentle lifting of the eyebrows or widening of the eyes, or a slight shifting closer or farther from your conversation partner that expresses the amount of excitement or intimacy of the conversation. When you are comfortable with this, add more consciousness of your non-word vocal expression. This includes *laughs*, *sighs*, and *exclamations* of surprise.

Practice using your voice instead of air sounds through your throat or nose such as huffing or snorting. Notice that when you laugh, it is possible to project it as a very pure vocal release, a little like singing. Notice what it's like to use restraint here, with just brief but clear laughter. Phase two of this practice is to choose responses that consciously contextualize what your conversation partner is communicating.

For example, get in touch with your most positive reaction to what they are saying and subtly adjust your body language and facial expressions to convey these positive reactions. It is as if you are somehow providing background music to their self-expression, but it is with your body instead of sound. If it is a very personal communication, you might foster in yourself a very empathic and understanding state, and saturate your subtle body language with that.

Once you are comfortable with this, phase three of your practice is to bring forward the state in yourself that, as background music or context, will influence your conversation partner's state in a direction that can be productive.

For example, if your friend does not feel understood in a situation and is taking it too seriously, you might exude understanding while at the same time, a feeling of being larger than the situation. If your friend is very sad, you might bring forward a combination of empathy and being resolved and at peace, as though you have experienced such losses and have found inner peace, but at the same time feel deeply what the other person's pain means. Phase four is to bring this system into your work with your clients. To do this, you must have a good sense of what kind of leading will be most productive.

Rather than trying to force things in a productive direction, think more short term, as in facilitating a state in your client that will foster a feeling that will pave the way toward progress. For example, if you have a client who is obsessed with having been betrayed by a lover, you can make space for them to vent; BUT, at the same time, promote a state in them which is about how *commonplace* such betrayals are, and how *complicated* people are, and *how your client has the capacity to betray as well.* This sensibility is useful because people with this expansive view of humanity and themselves make for a less dramatic and self obsessed experience of such a betrayal.

But what kind of state on your part might promote such expansion on their part?

You will find the answer to this in *Symbolic Somatic Priming*, which is an extension of the method you are reading now.

And what might your motives be for paving the way to this more expansive state?

You might prevent revenge that would harm someone, including your client. You can help them make objective decisions sooner than they might have if you were merely commiserating or expecting them to *"get over it and get to work."* You will also be promoting a healing state shift that can be part of reprocessing. State shifts can produce profound shifts in thinking.

People tend to focus on how changing thoughts can change their state. This is known as "*top down*" thinking. But a "*bottom up*" approach that emphasizes the power of more primal resources in influencing how we think is often even more powerful. By primal resources, we mean the "*older*" (from an evolutionary point of view) aspects of the nervous system that are mostly unconscious.

Symbolic Somatic Priming

Although there are many ways to convey or encourage feelings with gestures, this system highlights a style that conforms to some things that people commonly experience because of the biopsychological sources, encoding, and interpretation of emotion.

There is some cultural conditioning in emotion, even to the point that there are psychosomatic conditions that often appear in some cultures that are not evident in others, but this approach can easily be modified for the individual client or general culture. As you talk with your client, consider what emotions are affecting them, but that are not very conscious.

Of those, determine which ones you feel are especially good to give permission to be expressed. For example, a client may be trying to stay strong despite a grievous loss, while you know that they may fair better if they are able to share and express their feelings. Say a thing or two that shows your *appreciation* of their situation.

As you do this, include body language and a gesture that expresses the kind of feeling that you are giving permission to. Let's say that you are at a point where you want to show your awareness and understanding, and move the discussion toward finding out about how much support she has or how she has been doing. You might start by mentioning the shock of what happened. At that time, you might show a slight scrunching of the face while pulling your head back a bit, as if you were suddenly exposed to excessive light or heat. This conveys the shocking and difficult nature of initially realizing the loss. Again, this is a slight or *subtle* gesture.

As you say a word that expresses their connection with the loss (such as what they saw), you might relax your face with moderately open eyes and a slight nod as if to convey that you are unflinchingly prepared to discuss the loss without making the client feel responsible for your feelings or having to be indirect for your sake.

You are also working to prime the client for a state of freedom in addressing the loss in whatever way is needed. It's good to follow a move like that with an easy release of breath, triggering a release of tension in yourself in the hopes that this will activate some initial relaxation in your client's chest. This can lead to contact with emotions of grief, and with warm feelings for the person they are sharing their conversation with.

Then, you might connect this with the significance of the loss. (This way, you are moving from shock to the significance and challenge.

As a result, you will be in a better position to move to more assessment and perhaps a more general healing discussion about the person who was lost, since a more interventive NLP approach may not be appropriate at the most acute period of a traumatic or grief experience.) At that point, you might show a gently protective gesture, as if you were cupping your hands around your heart for a moment, while bending slightly at the solar plexus to convey a sense of caring as a grown up.

A slight sideways tilt of the head makes an even more non-threatening and understanding quality.

You might say:

"*Ooh,* (face scrunch and pull back, inhale so you can do the release in a moment) *you actually saw* (opening back up and slight nod, relaxed chest exhale) *the fatal crash. It's* (heart directed gesture, slight forward fold at solar plexus, head a little to the side) *hard enough to lose someone, not to mention... Well, can you tell me a little about who is with you to be supportive during all this? I know your daughter brought you in today.*"

Somatic Awareness Enhancement

This is very similar to the previous Symbolic Somatic Priming. However, this system serves to help the person feel a sense of flow through their body, to "fill in" areas that may feel less aware and alive, or to just connect with a particular area for some other awareness purpose. This can be good for aiding the state change that is a good part of reprocessing. When they are able to tolerate it, clients who are out of touch.

For example, a person who has experienced a difficult childhood may not be very aware of their heart area. When you are at a point in your relationship where the client can begin feeling that area, you might talk about what it means to *"reclaim feelings"* or to *"be more fully alive in your own body."*

At the same time, you can gently sweep your hands upward from the abdomen up through the heart area over the sternum. Since clients with difficult childhoods are often frightened by the feeling of emptiness where their heart should be, you can help them reclaim their awareness with such a gesture.

Of course, this is just part of a larger collection of interventions. In another example, when you're talking to a person who is prone to controlling others in order to protect his flagging self esteem, it can be helpful to connect him to the somatic experience that comprises the knee jerk response to feelings of insecurity. This feeling has become a reflex of anger and feeling justified in punishing the person who "made" them angry. This can be a formula for domestic violence. You might talk about how amazing it is that the body can go into a totally different state the moment someone says something that hits a nerve. As you do that, you might tense your chest and bring your fists up toward your chest while pulling your shoulders up into a tense position. Again, this can be a moderate or subtle gesture.

There is no reason for it to be extreme, because you are directing awareness, and this is easy to do with mild gestures that do not call to much attention to themselves and distract the client from the process you are conducting.

With the client more aware of how their body reacts, it will be easier to move into working on creating alternate responses. Again, with a serious issue, this is just one aspect of your communication and methods.

With the next few techniques, we will experience different paths to connecting with one's passionately held values and expressing them in a compelling manner. This can help your client focus in a more goal-oriented fashion, as well as derive more motivation and inspiration from their existing values and needs.

Essence

In earlier experiences, you connected your client with their values and vision. You may have even shared some of your *Word Punctuation methods* to help them speak in a more compelling manner. In the *Passion in Values*, you will help your client speak from their values and passion with the kind of economy of words that creates more impact. This is especially helpful with clients who have a lot to say about their problem, especially when they don't seem to have boiled things down very well in their own minds.

It's best for situations having to do with interpersonal controversy or efforts to formulate personal plans such as for career. The name of this system comes from its focus on leading with the essence, or core values and desires, of your message to yourself or others. As your client describes the details of their problem, reflect back what they are saying, but only the most essential parts. Be sure to include your best sense of what the client wants as an outcome for the situation.

See if the client feels that you are on target.

As you discuss these *"most essential parts,"* feed back to your client a very brief statement that sums up the most essential of the essential parts. As much as possible, bring to the foreground that which you feel will be useful in your work.

Incorporate the client's highest values and desires for the situation. See if you can create with your client a slogan that captures the essence of what you are bringing into focus. For example, a client had a husband with a narcissistic streak. She was coming to see that she was not helpless in the situation, and that the right leadership could improve his behavior and his understanding of her. Her counselor had some concern about whether this relationship would be tolerable in the long run, but he did not want to interfere with the client's freedom of choice, and there was no actual threat of harm to the client. So, in keeping with the ethical obligation of relationship therapists to honor their clients' choices for relationships *(for example, see the ethical guidelines of the American Association of Marriage and Family Therapists),* he satisfied himself with carefully assessing the client's motivation and awareness regarding the relationship. Since the assessment had taken place, and a good working relationship was beginning to form, the counselor used this system to come up with the following feedback:

"So I'm getting that you really want Jeff to show you he hears what you say, and will not play mind games like using legalistic arguments to talk you out of your honest feelings. And you want him to stop interfering with your choices, like your relationship with your best friend, Alicia."

This statement summarized about twenty-five minutes of explanation, not to mention the previous interaction. The client felt that this really captured how she felt. After a bit more chatting, the therapist offered up a tighter summary:

"Don't mess with me."

This got quite a reaction. The client flushed and became teary. She said, *"Oh my god, that's it. He really IS messing with me. I get in such a tangle trying to follow what he's saying, but I know he's just being manipulative at times like that! He really has been MESSING with me."*

The counselor was quick to help his client direct her anger into positive work. They spent the rest of the session coming up with ways to respond to her husband's manipulative ploys. He helped her stay in touch with her value of bringing out the best in everyone. This kept the session from veering into petty bitterness or pay back. The summary and slogan helped them stay in touch with her core desires.

For example, he taught her that attention reinforces behavior, so she should pay the most attention to his most gracious or non-narcissistic behavior. He helped her find some ways to minimize the attention she paid to his more manipulative behavior, and helped her find some terse responses that she could choose from when withdrawing her attention.

They came up with phrases like, *"You're just saying that,"* and *"talk to me when you want to be more understanding."* She also decided to confront her husband when is was failing to see her point of view with a phrase such as, *"You didn't actually take in what I'm saying, have you?"* and letting the question hang there without saying anything else. This strategy alone cause her husband to realize that he was not actually listening, because his own agenda was so strong in his mind that it blocked out what other's would say to him. It also helped her convince him to come in for some couples therapy, something he had vowed would never happen.

Somatic Leading

Leaders are good at choosing their words, but their message has more than a literary quality, compelling ideas, or brevity. Their speech is laced with the passion they feel for their mission. Their words embody their values by expression the feelings those values inspire in them. But leaders are not only those who command a big presence in world affairs or in organizations. Everyone has many opportunities for leadership in their everyday life.

> And leadership is not dominion over others; it is interactive and depends on trust.

Both members of a couple can lead according to their special contributions to the relationship, at least they can when their partner recognizes their gifts. Where one partner has common sense, the other may excel in creativity. Where one can be very assertive where bold moves are needed, the other may contribute most in very delicate matters that require subtle moves.

As you help your client connect with their values by using the methods of this book, also help them see how those values are expressed in their bodies. For example, you can ask the simple question, *"How do you know?"* followed by: *"I mean, how do you know you FEEL that way. Where does it live in your body, how do you know it's there; your values about this, your true values?"*

A client responded to this question with:

"Okay, I'm thinking of my boss actually going along with this idea, and how it will get us a lot of press and interest from major buyers. I can see us opening up new lines and taking this international. I feel almost like a beam of light coming out of my heart that kind of sweeps everything upwards into a new level."

This client had a *kinesthetic* and *visual* representation of their excitement. The counselor had the client stay in contact with this feeling and image while pretending to tell her boss about her idea. She practiced giving a voice to her feelings. At first, she choked up, because she wasn't used to allowing her feelings to come out like this. She realized that she had learned to use a lot of restrained when communicating in order to play it safe.

This has its advantages in the corporate world, but she realized that this was not a good idea when she had an opportunity to inspire. The counselor had her practice this whenever she was driving in her car, and to record it and fine-tune her presentation so until she could switch her inspiration and voice on at will. They also supported this goal with some NLP state management and visualization work.

Vision Communication Protocol

All too often, the stereotype of the male becoming overwhelmed and withdrawn or angry when his mate confronts him with more emotional issues than he is prepared to cope with at one time plays out in relationships. Of course, males don't have a complete monopoly on this trait. But, more commonly, women find it difficult to cope with the male *"Mr. Fixit"* approach to problems, which women say squeezes out their need for process and deeper understanding.

This protocol directly resolves this problem on several levels. It sets up a frame fr a new approach, it provides mental and temporal space for the protocol to do its magic, and it grounds the participants in a manner that greatly reduces the anxiety that is the cause of so much communication dysfunction.

Frame the situation by explaining to the woman that the male has a very small *emotion bladder* in their brain. Women find this amusing because they or one of their friends may have complained of having a small urinary bladder. If you're talking to a man, explain that females are not usually as good at mechanical reasoning as men, and can have trouble designing their emotional issues into a workable arrangement.

Men find this amusing, because they have seen their mate or other women have trouble with mechanical reasoning of some kind; perhaps something concerning the physics of operating a motor vehicle. I hope you'll forgive the appeal to stereotypes, but I am concerned with *what works* and what maintains rapport and momentum in the therapeutic relationship more than being completely politically correct at all times. This framing works just as well when working with homosexual partners, since both genders are typically able to take their own peccadilloes lightly. For your ill-humored clients, you may want to use a very neutral way to introduce this protocol. Explain that the protocol allows people to bring up very serious issues in a positive way that does not tend to alienate or overwhelm people, and avoids coming off as a *Mr. Fixit* mentality.

Describe the protocol as follows:

The client is to select the most important emotional issue, rather than overwhelm or confuse their partner by daisy-chaining the issues.

Daisy-chaining happens when a person thinks of a disturbing issue, develops a state that causes them to think of one related issue after the other, verbalize them as they come to mind, and overwhelm, confuse, or antagonize their partner as a result.

With this single most important issue in mind, have the person think of what the relationship would be like if the issue was resolved in a meaningful, generative way. Then, have the person describe the values that make this outcome meaningful to them.

Work with your client to think up the kinds of steps that would move their relationship toward that vision. These steps must be realistic, practical, and as attractive as possible. They should be worded in the most inspirational way possible. They should then be reworked so that they appeal to the mindset and speech style of the partner. This step can feel pleasantly subversive to your client, who is used to feeling some futility and frustration because they have confused being genuine with limiting their speech to their own frame of reference.

Breaking out of this self-imposed habitual limitation can seem somehow like cheating. It's important to keep the process fun so the person does not lose momentum by thinking that they really are cheating in some way. Now work with your client to come up with a single step that would move the relationship into this plan.

It should be something that can be done almost immediately. Note that by doing this step last in formulating the plan, your client is more likely to come up with a meaningful item than if they start out with an effort to come up with the step.

This is because they have stepped back to look at the big picture, thinking of their long-term desires and their overarching values, even if only briefly.

Now have them practice communicating this in the following sequence:

1) The set up: *"I know you know how important you are to me, and the kind of vision we share for our relationship. I mean, I see us* (vision goes here)."

2) *"This means so much to me, because I value* (one or two values go here)."

3) *"And I know we can create this by doing things like* (one to three steps go here)."

4) *"I'd just love it if you could join with me in moving us closer to that by* (very easy initial step goes here; your client is asking for a simple behavior that would mean a lot to him or her in the relationship, and it must be something the partner is definitely able to do)."

Here is a real life example from a client (the real names were changed, of course):

"Bill, I know you love me. There are so many ways that you show me that. Even the little things you do like the way you make breakfast on Saturdays. And I know

you want to see us having our talks be easier and get to positive places without a lot of hassle."

Note that the client, *Ellen*, is reframing very hard in the direction of her mate's perspective here. Otherwise, she might be saying she really wants their discussions to be more productive and for him to show that he really understands and cares about what she is bringing up, etc.

"I think if we worked out at the gym together a couple times a week this would be great for us, because we don't want to let our work and money issues to get to us. You know how much sharper we are and how much more stamina we have when we get on our game that way."

If she were not framing this in his terms, she might be saying that they need to spend more time together and work through issues more; the sex would be better if he were in better shape and she's embarrassed about getting flabby, and she knows he doesn't really like her body these days; in the car, they could talk back and forth from the gym and get closer; she really has a hard time just going to the gym on her own and needs support to exercise regularly; she's been feeling kind of depressed and needs him to be more positive and uplifting so she can feel better about doing more things, etc.

"You could really help me if you could schedule your appointments so we can rely on Wednesday nights and Saturdays later in the morning. I know you want

to keep Saturday afternoons and some evenings open for work. How does that sound?" (Face relaxed with a little smile, head tilted a little to the side.)

Please note that this is in no way intended to suppress discussion of serious issues such as depression, weight loss, mutual support, the emotional tone of a relationship, sex quality, body image, working through issues productively, and discussing issues adequately - all things that were brought up in the parenthetical remarks about the client reframing what she might have said.

The point is that, at this point in the relationship, her approach and his response have been disastrous, while this protocol has saved many couples by giving them a structure to work on issues productively and without becoming too triggered. If you think of a relationship as something that requires conditioning over time, like an athlete's body or a scientist's mind, then working through issues with quality in a step-wise fashion that is tied to big picture values and vision can be a positive one.

A counter-argument might be that relationships must be approached holistically, so pulling out a single desire fails to address ecology. But remember, the single desire was derived after looking holistically at the relationship, and was the highest priority out of a number of things that would be supportive from a holistic perspective.

Success with one item can galvanize the couple to continue this process over time, with additional successes adding up to the vision they are pursuing together. On the other hand, when this gambit fails, it will be much clear where the problem lies, or what dynamic is taking place, because of the way the issues have been isolated and framed. For example, if the partner has too much dissociation and regression to tolerate even a single request that is framed so positively, that partner requires mental health care that addresses this problem. The same would apply to a partner who is too compromised by drugs or alcohol to follow through adequately, even though the discussion went well at the time.

Matrixing in Problem Formulation and Planning

Matrixing is a way to strategically plan your work. It uses NLP to generate your responses to the client on the fly. This means we can use NLP know how such as analyzing the client's meta-programs and repairing their meta-model violations. If you aren't 100% on top of things like meta-model violations, the processes to follow will still make sense.

Quick Review: Meta-Programs and Meta-Model

If you're new to meta programs or interested in learning this subject thoroughly and in a practical manner, read the book: "**NLP: The 57 Meta-Programs**" (ISBN- 8087518071).

In case you only need a short reminder, *meta-programs* are the cognitive patterns that an individual tends to emphasize in managing their mental processes. This establishes an important link between our thoughts and the sensory representations that NLP uses in so much of its work. You could say that meta-programs are the rules that govern our thought and decision-making patterns, especially in terms of how we select from our memories and environment in triggering and constructing those patterns.

Put more concisely, meta-programs constitute the rules by which we select strategies (mental, behavioral, etc.) that we use to achieve our outcomes.

One way to get a feel for someone's meta-programs is to notice what they pay attention to. An example meta-program is **"toward versus away from."**

A "*toward*" meta-program derives motivation and perspective from moving toward something. A person on a diet would experience himself or herself moving *toward* their desired weight and appropriate foods.

An "*away from*" strategy would emphasize eliminating fat and *avoiding* fattening foods or excessive eating. The meta-model asserts that we must exclude a great deal of information in order to function. When this exclusion takes place in a dysfunctional way, it can lead to problems such as overgeneralizing, as in bigotry. Such errors are called meta-model violations.

One method of repairing such violations is to ask questions that require a more specific answer or that bring forth a contradiction. For example:

"If atheists are immoral, how do you explain this long list of atheists who have made great contributions to humanity?" or... *"You say she hates you? What exactly do you mean by hate? I know she did you a favor yesterday."*

Matrixing for Complicated Problems

Matrixing means being relevant to complicated problems requiring a strategic response, rather than a formulaic one. This is in contrast to a common approach of NLP practitioners, which is to focus on a very specific problem, and apply a specific technique to the problem. This is not to say that such an approach is wrong. There can be great benefit to the artful winnowing down of a vague problem into a specific, operational definition, and many NLP practitioners excel at this.

Many of them also excel at selecting a technique from their NLP quiver to rapidly resolve the problem. However, not every person will receive adequate help if their problem must be the equivalent of a sliver in their finger, and there's no reason to limit NLP's contribution to that of a pair of tweezers. Many of the problems clinicians and coaches find are quite complicated. Some coaching clients may seem to have buried themselves in unresourceful narratives and stories that they have become very attached to. Many clients will work with a coach on success or other life issues, but have mild mental health issues that are either left over after getting psychotherapy, or that have not been bad enough to get the client to see a therapist.

The book **Shadow Syndromes** talks about the way that *"subclinical"* issues can disrupt peoples' lives without necessarily being readily diagnosable. We often call these clients *"twilight"* clients, because they may benefit from psychotherapy or medication, but are not necessarily motivated to explore that route. When they are, their residual problems don't contraindicate coaching, but they can make them more challenging to the coach. Because such problems affect nearly everyone in some way, coaches should get to know enough psychopathology to help them understand their more stuck or confusing clients. This knowledge can be useful in many ways. It can help the coach respond in a more strategic way and help them have a more realistic sense of what will be needed.

Favorite Matrix

I'm tempted to call this a starter matrix, but it is so fundamental to thinking about problems. This matrix may look simple, but it is very flexible and can be used to formulate very complicated problems, especially if you use it in a mind map format. You can use it for an overview of all the life needs of a client, or use it to zero in on a specific problem. It supports holistic and strategic planning. It helps to bring your intent and next best actions into focus. Let's start with the categories, and then an example. The Four Categories:

Meaning:

Examples include stigma, self concept. vision as a source of goals, and meta-model violations.

Context:

People, things, and situations in the person's environment that affect them.

Behavior:

The actual behavior of the person, and any plans that have a strong emphases directly on behavior, such as behavior modification. Can include desired behavioral goals and habits. Can focus on ways that developmental issues have created behavior limitations or patterns.

Physiology:

A focus on what is affecting the client from a biological perspective. Can include lifestyle factors such as exercise and diet. The more you think in terms of evolutionary psychology and the "internal pressures" that this creates, the more you may find yourself thinking in terms of physiology. As you know, NLP has plenty to say about observing and influencing your client's physiology, while thinking in terms of state management. Both coaches and therapists find that they can think more about physiology as they incorporate reprocessing techniques such as EMDR and EFT into their work.

Now Try This:

Think of a client, or even yourself. On a fresh, blank sheet of paper (or some kind of mind mapping software) put the four categories near the center.

From there, you can branch out and add the most important related issues. Continue to branch out until you have actionable items.

Here's an example (*The name and some of the details have been changed to protect her privacy):*

Marcy is 30, hates her job, loves her husband, hates they way they get into arguments, feels kind of untrusting and judgmental of people, is very bright, is a really good sales person, is underemployed because her employer isn't making very good use of her, and really wants to take her life to another level. She has trouble when a lot of little tasks and details come her way because of ADD. She has had counseling for ADD and has been reticent to take medication because it seems kind of creepy to her.

Meaning

Mary is generally irked. The underemployment, overwhelm with details, and feeling intolerant of people that act petty, boring, or stupid, all make life less satisfying.

She loves her husband, but he thinks and speaks in a very step-wise fashion.

This is very difficult to tolerate for a person who thinks in hypertext. She realizes, though, that he is bright and successful, and his heart is in the right place. Coaching or counseling will need to help her find a more life-affirming and dynamic way to be a very smart person in a world that can seem pretty dumb.

Context

Her need to improve her career is important here, because her context is a major source of her complaints. The results will show up here, but this is not necessarily the category where the real action will be.

Changes in her attitude (*Meaning*), and strategies (*Behavior*) may be the keys that unlock her career potential, or help her convince her employer to make better use of her sales skills, which are excellent.

Behavior

Her issues with the rest of humanity show up here in the sense that she does not have very satisfying relationships in her personal life, and she is not sure how to get into harmony with her husband. In addition to working in the Meaning category, behavioral strategies may be important.

Physiology

Marcy has a lot of youthful energy, but the issues are taking their toll. Nonetheless, she brings a lot of energy to her job, her relationship, and her home projects. ADD has a physiological side, of course, and she will need to learn to cope with it, even if she takes medication. ADD coping methods will go in the behavior category. The prospect of medication, supplements, and other things that address ADD from a physiological angle go here.

How a Treatment Plan Would Look

Here is an example of a plan for someone like Marcy. She has come in for coaching. She has had psychotherapy, and it has been helpful, but she wants to focus on success and lifestyle. Nonetheless, it if very obvious that there are emotional issues and ADD symptoms that loom large.

Meaning

Goals: *To get from irked to fun and strategic.* Getting into harmony with people and her husband. By being feed up from her distracting judgmentality and impatience, she will probably come up with better strategies for making her relationships more satisfying. By being less distracted by feeling oppressed and under-appreciated at work, she will probably be able to come up with better strategies for her career as well.

Methods: Metaphoric, reframing and other counseling techniques will be helpful. Reprocessing will be more helpful if we can connect with earlier experience that helped to establish her pattern of relating. Timeline work might be very helpful here.

Context

Goals: *To get from overwhelmed and under-appreciated to meaningful challenges that draw upon her gifts and inspire her to develop even higher skills.*

Methods: Sometimes it is necessary to get context changes in order to progress in coaching or counseling. In this case, it looks like the context change is a goal rather than a short-term objective. That means that the focus on methods will be in the other categories. Not that keeping an eye on the classifieds isn't a good idea.

Behavior

Goals: *Round out her success with targeted strategies.*

The first two sessions created a strong impression that the short-term action is in the meaning and physiology areas. **Methods:** Coming in a close third is the area of ADD coping strategies.

> These strategies will probably do a lot for her attitude and feelings of resourcefulness as well.

This should create an upward, self-reinforcing spiral. It is also be important to add to her intimacy skills with her husband. But her thought patterns that bind her into less resourceful ways of handling her husband come first.

Physiology

Goals: *Reduce ADD symptoms and respond to old emotional triggers from a state of fresh mastery.*

Methods: Consider medication (via a referral to a psychiatrist), supplements, exercise, and anything else that will help her with ADD from a physiological perspective. Direct her to sources of information for this. Do reprocessing to help her generate a more resourceful state instead of being stuck in the irked state. NLP techniques will rely a great deal on state management during whatever processes are used.

Momentum

In any coaching or therapy, momentum is very important. By momentum, we mean that a productive process is taking place at the correct tempo. Since NLP relies on state management much of the time, and since states are dynamic processes, the pace of the steps in the intervention must be maintained. In this section, we are going to show some examples of that kind of work, and this will take place in the context of moving clients into a context of their own higher values. We will begin with a deconstruction process that helps loosen their grip on habitual thinking and feeling patterns. Then we will "reconstruct" into work dedicated to excellence and higher values.

Deconstructing Into Modalities

This key and basic move can allow you to move in a number of directions. It is an excellent set up for a reframe, for reprocessing, and as part of a hypnotic induction.

In this pattern, we ask a simple question, *"How do you know that you..."* and guide the client into experiencing the sense modalities that make up their knowledge.

This converts knowledge into something that can be questioned, added to, reformulated, deducted from, and made more dynamic. It can help identify illogic that the client can begin to question on their own, thus "owning" their experience with no incentive to resist the therapists "*agenda*." It is an excellent gateway to body awareness patterns, because senses are, well, senses.

It helps the client become less attached to their mental narrative, acting somewhat like oil for a squeaky hinge. This is one of those sub-patterns that I mentioned in the introduction. It is a fragment of a larger, strategic series of moves. You'll get some additional ideas about what to do with the results later in this section.

Example I

Client: *"I feel like such a complete loser."*

Therapist: *"How do you know that?"*

Client: *"Well, it's pretty clear when you have friends that..."*

Therapist: *"Wait, I mean how do you know that you feel like a loser. How does it feel?"*

Client: *"Totally awful, I feel like giving up."*

Therapist: "Where do you feel that in your body? Where is the main center of that feeling, of the emotion or intensity?"

Client: *"Well, really, it's like my stomach is twisted up."*

Example II

Client: *"I just can't do it. I can't face him, much less make any sense."*

Therapist: *"As you think about doing that, or, I mean, not doing that, how do you feel if you were looking at him and trying to make sense?"*

Saying *"or, I mean, not doing that,"* helps to forestall an objection such as, *"But I can't,"* so you can maintain your momentum. Also notice the use of conjugations, mixing, *"how do you feel,"* an *"if"* phrase, and, *"trying to make sense."*

Client: *"I would be shut down. I really hate him."*

Therapist: *"So if you're facing him and shut down, where is that feeling of being shut down? Where do you feel it mostly?"*

Client: *"All over. I just want to turn and go."*

Therapist: *"So there is a motivation to action, to move, to escape. What is that like?"*

Client: *"Oh, well, I would probably feel panicky. Either that or start yelling at him."*

Therapist: *"And where is the center of that feeling? Your heart? Your throat?"*

Client: *"It just moves right up through me from my heart."*

Reconstructing Into Values

Our culture doesn't encourage people to articulate their values or even to introspect very much. Our social institutions, including our schools, and major media outlets tend to encourage thinking in cliches.

> You really help clients develop an entirely new level of self-respect and appreciation when you link their automatic thoughts and efforts to their highest values.

Then they get the added benefit of seeing how they can become even more aligned. If there's anything an NLP practitioner knows, it's that alignment creates more creativity and energy than most people knew they had.

When you deconstruct the client's experience through a process such as the previous one, or some other sense mode breakdown, you are in a good position to work toward reconstruction.

Example

Therapist: *"So you really want to say these things to him, and you know that with his personality, he will start manipulating and not really let it register. At least that's his usual style. Tell me about the values that drive your desire to say these things."*

Client: *"Well, it's really disturbing to know he's in this little world of his pulling something like this with no accountability. I really want to get through to him."*

Therapist: *"If you got through to him, that would mean that he would be a more caring person who could contribute more to the world, I suppose."*

Client: "Well, yes. "

Therapist: *"Oh, and you would feel very different, free to say what you want and improvise when someone plays games like that. "*

Client: *"Yes, I have to say I feel limited with people like that. I seem to attract these idiots. Each time I'm angrier than the last time."*

Therapist: *"I suppose you could say that your desire to meet a challenge like this is about making the world a better place."*

Client: *"Okay, yeah, that would feel good. When pigs fly."*

Therapist: *"So do you doubt your ability to communicate your values, or his ability to hear them?"*

Client: "*Well, I'm sure with a little work I could be ready to say what I need to say. But this guy is a real piece of work. I don't think anybody ever gets through to him.*"

Therapist: "*Does that mean that refocusing your efforts on your own goals would be more meaningful than this fellow's personality problem?*"

Client: "*Okay, yeah, you got that right. It's true. I should.*"

Therapist: "*Since you tensed up and seemed unhappy about that prospect, let's talk a little about what makes this not inspire you -- because I know you get very jazzed about certain kinds of professional challenges.*"

Note that we are starting to trigger a more resourceful state, by comparing this challenge to some that have inspired her, and by reminding her of feeling inspired. From here, the work would be about resolving obstacles to letting go of people with certain types of personalities, and on how to strategically cope with them, perhaps in terms of office politics. The *"reconstructing into values"* here is that the client is thinking in terms of pursuing higher values at the same time as communicating more effectively. This helps make the work about something better than getting revenge or obsessing.

Future Now

The following is a way to help your client clarify their priorities, and focus their commitments to working on their issues. Ask your client if they're up for a little experiment that will not take too long. Ask them to imagine that it is one year (or an interval of your choice) in the future, and that you would like to do your session on that day, only now. The client pretends to be seeing you for help with challenges that could be occurring a year from now. You can improvise this to emphasize themes that your client can benefit from.

A likely benefit is that the client will have a dramatic shift in their perception of what the real priorities are. Some things will become nuisances that are going to fade into the past without a lot of worry, while others that were neglected become of supreme importance.

> If the client is working with you on a positive future, you can emphasize their skilled use of resources over the past imaginary year.

But you can also help them realize that they can benefit from setting much more profound goals. If they paint a dark picture, you can help them identify priorities. Then they can realize that they have "gained" a year and start working on them a year ago, before your imaginary present.

Vision Down-Stream

This simple method has produced some really marvelous results in relationships that have become strained and alienated. It a great way to cross a gender or personality gap for nearly any two personality types.You already know about the importance of establishing a secure base for pretty much anything to happen in a relationship. You also know that alignment means that your values are lined up with you behavior. At least that's one good version of alignment.

> This approach to communication involves creating secure base as well as alignment.

It also adds in some good old-fashioned sales sense. This approach to communicating is to be taught to your client. You can also use it to get important ideas across to your clients. The people who respond best seem to be the type who are moved by vision and values, and the type that think like engineers, who like to see the plan in an organized way. However, it is good for almost any type of person.

Have your client tell you about the problem that they need to communicate to their friend about (or their spouse, employer, or whoever). Have them describe the point of being concerned about this. Instead of trying to get what they are "really" trying to say, have them describe what would happen if they got it across and the other person responded well. We don't mean the short-term outcome of ending the conversation on nice terms. We mean the result of a collaborative relationship that got meaningful results regarding the issue at hand.

For example, if your client is tired of walking on eggshells around her husband, ask how she would know that the issue was collaboratively resolved. Go beyond the obvious matter of her being able to speak her mind freely. Have her describe some of her husband's behaviors in this ideal future scenario. Next, ask what vision and values this outcome would express. She might say that she would feel more relaxed and loving, and that the things they want to do together would work out better because there would be more (and more effective) communication. They would collaborate more, so there would be more constructive effort producing results in their lives.

To make this more motivational, have her tell you about some of these results, because they will reflect the dreams she has for the relationship in terms of lifestyle and activities she longs for.

Now help her compress this down into specific values that are more abstract. They might be the following:

1) Freedom of expression (knowing the other person will really try to understand the positive intent behind what you say);

2) Mutual respect (knowing that your contribution to the relationship will be valued and supported);

3) Constructive collaboration (happily working together);

4) Realizing our dreams (being able to achieve and experience the things we long for).

It really doesn't matter if client after client comes up with pretty much the same values for their relationship. These needs are universal. Often, spelled out, they sound a little like parts of the U.S. Constitution.

Now have your client describe the medium-term goals that would be aligned with the longer-term vision and values. And next have her tell you what she'd like to see happen in the short term, especially in terms of how her husband can help her begin moving toward the medium-term objectives.

Okay, *now* we have vision and values aligned with objectives and tasks. That is, the big picture and the worm's-eye view. Now help her practice initiating the conversation with her husband.

These things always go better if a person can start of with canned material. It gives them some confidence and momentum, and helps them command attention and interest because they will express themselves in a more grounded way.

Finally, have her try this out with her husband, and work with her based on the results she gets. By the way, we are talking here about a reasonably functional relationship. If her husband is a highly manipulative person, we would not necessarily try this. We might choose to be focused more on training the husband with behavior modification.

Reprocessing

Reprocessing is a very powerful ingredient for bringing out more of the potential in coaching and therapy. It's very important to understand *reprocessing*, because it is a key to the success of many therapy techniques, including a lot of NLP processes. In fact, once you understand it, you'll realize it's been hiding in plain sight. Reprocessing happens when we take a badly encoded experience (or set of experiences) and re-encode them. As a result, we can be more successful, and less reactive. Symptoms such as panic, anxiety, sleep problems, and compulsive thoughts, are alleviated.

At its simplest, you could say that reprocessing helps us eliminate symptoms and become more successful after overwhelming experiences.

People naturally turn experience into success, and we naturally regain our balance after an overwhelming experience. We do a lot of that during REM sleep. *It's a natural process.* However, when this does not happen, we can be in serious mental health trouble. When an experience is too overwhelming, our bodies may not be able to encode it properly. *Dysregulation* of brain functions may result along with poor sleep. This can lead to worsening breakdown into full-blown post-traumatic stress disorder (PTSD). You already know that NLP can help people change how they represent things so that they can experience them and respond successfully. Perhaps the best-known NLP process for doing that with past experiences is *Time Line Therapy* ™, originated by the famous NLP master trainer, Tad James.

Throughout the history of psychotherapy, there were occasional experiences of dramatic reductions in anxiety or trauma symptoms, but it was not until EMDR came along that the field of psychotherapy as a whole came to think of rapid resolution such symptoms as being fairly commonplace, and that took a good number of years to take place even then.

There were other techniques that were available prior to EMDR, but they had not gained widespread acceptance. The NLP phobia *cure* and *visual kinesthetic dissociation* are examples from NLP. Thought field therapy (TFT) is another, and was an early energy psychology technique.

Once you **deconstruct** reprocessing, you can find it in other traditions such as religions. Some of the *"tech"* from Scientology causes reprocessing. If reprocessing happens in a religious experience, the credit is given to the religion (or God) and can be used as an indoctrination tool, and when it happens in energy psychology such as TFT or emotional freedom technique (EFT), energy flow and balance are given the credit. As brain science progresses, scientists are getting a better understanding of how this happens from a physiological perspective.

> Understanding reprocessing is kind of like knowing the combination to a lock.

For a very long time, therapists have worked with processes such as emotional catharsis, visualization and hypnosis, occasionally triggering reprocessing, but not realizing how to go about it systematically for a more consistent result. The goal of this next section is to help you not only recognize it, but to tweak the techniques you use so that you can trigger it more effectively. We call this *"reprocessing on purpose."*

Reprocessing in the Field

Reprocessing can be done in a very stripped-down way, using its most core elements. EFT is a self-help technique that fits this description. Reprocessing can also be done through a much richer, well-rounded psychotherapy process. EMDR fits this description. And, finally, Reprocessing can be achieved as part of a process that is not as focused on reprocessing. This happens when you are doing a process with a client, and you sequence it in such a way as to trigger reprocessing as part of the process.

Sometimes, experiences hit us in such a way as to trigger reprocessing. Sometimes, it just takes time for us to heal from an experience enough to start feeling like our old selves.

Most likely, though, reprocessing on purpose would have helped to restore us faster and perhaps with more wisdom as well. We should point out why you haven't heard more about it. First, many developers of techniques have come about it intuitively, and don't fully, consciously realize that they are using it.

Of course, this is not a new kind of observation.

From the beginnings of NLP, modelers were able to show therapists technical aspects of their work that the therapists were not conscious of. *Milton Erickson* famously said that he did not consciously understand a lot of what he did. *Virginia Satir* did not realize how much she depended on mirroring to establish rapport.

Similarly, many technique developers focus your attention on other elements of the technique, and fail to give credit to the reprocessing aspect.

Yet another is that many developers are tempted to draw a mote around their techniques, name the technique, and "*own*" it without recognizing what it has in common with other methods that get similar results.

> Reprocessing doesn't necessarily feel like anything is happening, even when you're wide-awake.

The best way to know if you have experienced it is if your symptoms go away and you find yourself responding to trigger situations in a balanced way. *Otherwise, what would be the point?*

Sometimes, the material being reprocessed is intense, and the person experiences emotional catharsis. Some people are convinced that they met a deceased person and it was profoundly healing.

Others experience it under hypnosis. If you know what to look for, you might notice that your thinking is more fluid. Many people experiencing reprocessing are able to see connections between their experiences and their issues more easily. They may feel the emotional charge of an issue dissipate.

The therapist may direct their attention to what is going on so that the experience has more validity for them. More importantly, tracking the before and after is important. During the assessment, collect information such as the frequency and situations of panic attacks or whatever the symptoms are.

Think Physiology

NLP is known for thinking *about* physiology. Usually, when NLP tells you to look at a person's physiology, it is telling you to get clues about their state, their congruence, and their unconscious. Since the beginnings of NLP, we know a great deal more about the nervous system and what causes people to become dysfunctional. This a very important area of knowledge to add to our skills. This is not just for academic interest, or for convincing clients of anything.

Along with our burgeoning knowledge of neurophysiology, we are also refining and even developing techniques based on this knowledge.

We are able to assess the effectiveness of techniques now by how well they "switch on" brain regions that have shut down. This is not only very persuasive data; it also allows researchers another avenue for vetting therapy methods that is less costly than extensive assessments of functioning over time *(although, ultimately, functioning and feeling good are the bottom line factors).*

So I'd like you to consider a few brain regions that get affected by trauma, and how a person is affected by these shut downs:

1) Memory problems resulting from shrinkage of the hippocampus.

2) Problems with forethought and problem solving resulting from reduction in frontal lobe functioning and excessive limbic system reactivity.

3) Reduced medial prefrontal cortex response means there is less control of fear responses with the prefrontal cortex exerting less control over the amygdala. This can also mean less efficient thinking and intrusive memories.

4) Excessive activation of the brain that interferes with REM sleep resulting from hormonal and other effects upon the adrenal-pituitary axis. REM sleep is essential for brain integrity. Without this, there is loss of coordination, reactions, anger control, mental clarity, and, eventually, life itself.

> Traumatized people tend to tell their story in a *chronological* order.

They don't tend to have it put together in terms of the big picture or in terms of philosophical meaning. When they do, it tends to be in a crude and troubling way. They can be very boring, because they have to work through stories step by step, without the aid of the big picture.

These brain issues are the cause of this kind of problem. But after successful treatment, brain scans show that the affected brain areas are switched on or toned down, depending on the imbalance. The resulting behavior, life successes, and ability to communicate that we see from people treated successfully are priceless. The moral of the story:

> Whenever you assess a client, think physiology. You'll have a much better idea of what you're dealing with. It is not enough to just think in terms of behavior and thoughts to wave your magic wand of NLP over.

Many of the clients that NLP practitioners give up on or consider to be poor participants are those who most need help because of brain shut downs. We must not give up on or judge people whose brains are not functioning properly. These people need us to have the proper skills, or the integrity to refer them to the appropriate specialists. Once you know the active ingredients of reprocessing, you'll begin to recognize it in various NLP techniques and elsewhere.

Targeting

Targeting means focusing awareness on something. In reprocessing, this may be a memory, thought, physical feeling, or emotion. Depending on how in-depth the reprocessing work is, an extensive assessment may have preceded this first step into reprocessing. In psychotherapy, many clients will need to do preliminary work in order to tolerate the work. This is most likely to be true for people with dissociation or serious childhood trauma histories. In EFT, this happens during the initial set up.

The State Shift

Once the person is focused on their issue, they experience a shift into a more relaxed and positive state. This can be accomplished in various ways. In EFT, the person taps acupuncture points and does eye movement patterns while maintaining the targeting. For more challenging cases, there can be added complications that challenge getting to this more positive state. For these people, a stripped down version will not typically be sufficient. However, people have used EFT for some surprisingly difficult problems.

Alternating Bilateral Stimulus:

One of the ways to help a state shift take place is to use a bilateral stimulus such as EMDR's eye movement (also used in EFT and TFT), sound or touch. *Basically, it directs attention from side to side.*

Mindfulness or Distraction:

Cultivating mindfulness, in which the client is able to just notice without feeling like they have to do anything, can help them shift into the positive state. EMDR therapists use language such as, *"Follow the light back and forth...go with that...where does that take you?"* In EFT, the client is occupied with tapping and a more complicated eye movement pattern that occupies their mind.

Cognitive Work

For many problems, working on thought patterns seems to be optional. For a psychotherapist, this is a little hard to swallow. But it appears that our states can affect our thoughts as much as our thoughts can affect our thoughts. It is remarkable to see how much thought patterns can change after a process as simple as EFT. However, it can be very productive to do cognitive work in the course of reprocessing. In EMDR, the client is helped to find the negative cognition that represents their poorly encoded experience.

For example, the client may realize that they have been carrying around the feeling and unconscious belief that they are helpless, because of how they felt in a traumatic situation. They are also helped to create a positive cognition that represents recovery from the negative one. That might be, *"I am an adult now, and the bad person is gone."* The transition into the positive cognition may be as simple as noticing how much more true it feels as various targets (such as traumatic memories and the negative beliefs themselves) are targeted and reprocessed.

Body Scan and Future Pacing

In some reprocessing, including EMDR, it is typical to have the person scan their body with their mind so that they can fully experience what it is like to have a positive state. Also, this may help them find additional imbalances to reprocess.

Future pacing is a way to project into the future how the new thought patterns and feelings will manifest. This can help to reinforce a more confident and masterful identity, as well as help the client create more meaningful goals.

Recovery (Longer-Term Status)

This is the most neglected phase of reprocessing in the methods that I'm familiar with. It is very important to remember that many clients have enduring physical problems as a result of PTSD, drug abuse, head injuries, and other problems with medical consequences. Consider sleep issues. If the person is not able to sleep effectively, they will not be able to fully recover, and may relapse into symptoms.

A person can sleep eight hours a night without sleeping effectively. Because of traumatic material that is to triggering, they may not make it through enough REM sleep. That's because REM sleep is where we try to reprocess that material naturally. If we were always able to do that, we might not need these reprocessing techniques.

Sleep normalization is a high priority.

Other physical areas may be medication stabilization and monitoring, coping with medication side effects, and cognitive rehabilitation that helps restore the client's ability to think effectively as they recover from brain injury. Brain injury may be caused by poor sleep, sleep apnea, strokes (even so-called *"silent strokes*" that may go undiagnosed), and seemingly slight impacts to the head. The need for cognitive rehabilitation is currently one of the biggest gaps in mental health care.

Time Line Therapy and Reprocessing

In this section, we will look at Time Line Therapy ™ from the perspective of *reprocessing*. This will show us how reprocessing experiences along the timeline can help people refine their thinking and respond more effectively. We will also draw from cognitive behavioral therapy.

This structure can be good for expediting personal growth, processing the little "t" traumas in our lives, or working with more challenging issues. People can become much more successful and at ease from processing a good number of small traumas. First, we'll run through this process without specific examples. Then we will do the full process for a case example. You'll notice that this is a summary of Time Line Therapy ™ that shows how to integrate reprocessing. **If you don't already know Time Line Therapy ™, I encourage you to learn it in depth.**

Bad Code

A cognitive therapist might call it a dysfunctional or irrational cognition. And EMDR therapist might call it a negative cognition. We like to call it *bad code*, because this highlights the fact that we make decisions about the world and ourselves when we go through experiences, especially intense, traumatic, or otherwise overwhelming experiences.

Most of us have "encoded" some of these experiences in an immature way, because we weren't ready for them. Unfortunately, these decisions about the world or about ourselves become part of our reality, like water to a fish; unquestioned.

Just as a computer doesn't question the code that runs it, we are driven to some degree by irrational decisions made under duress.

The place where these decisions reside is called implicit memory. We call it *"sticky memory"* because implicit memory is unconscious and unquestioned. It is simply the "*truth*."

In essence, bad code is the unwise perspective that you get from an experience that you weren't ready for.

If you had been fully ready for the experience, it would already be wisdom and you wouldn't be in therapy for it.

Good Code

If you learn from an experience, then you have made "*good code*" out of it.

When you reprocess bad code into rational or functional thinking, then you have converted bad code into good code.

Code Triggers

You know about triggers. In this approach, we are talking about triggers of bad code. This can be any situation that bears some similarity to the one that generated the bad code. It may not look like the situation; it need only have similar implications or meaning.

Source Event

As in Time Line Therapy ™, *reprocessing* may have its best impact when we go back to the situation that occurred first in causing you to create the bad code. At the most simple level, you would reprocess the experience using whatever reprocessing tools you felt were most appropriate. You would help your client move from bad code to good code, using whatever cognitive therapy skills were applicable.

Echo Events

These are things that resemble the source event and that reinforced or compounded the *bad code*. They are more influential than mere trigger events, because they are more overwhelming or happened at an early enough age to help form and strengthen bad code in important ways.

Future Success

These are what I like to call imaginary memories of the future. That is, future imaginings that help to build the client's sense of hope, meaning, and ability.

State-Initiated Reprocessing

Sometimes, with reprocessing, this happens as if by magic, with little intervention at a cognitive level. The greater share of the work might be in helping the client know what and how to target, rather than how to refine their thoughts about it.

In other words, the things you do to trigger reprocessing may not need to include cognitive therapy in order to get a profound cognitive shift. It depends on the client and the issue you are working on.

Skills

Whatever skills your client needs to learn for relationships, self-care, or whatever, they are best learned after their source and echo events are reprocessed. This is because trauma and overwhelm cause lasting shut downs of parts of the brain. This affects learning and memory, especially where touchy issues are concerned.

Bad Code:

Your client tells you that her relationships are not very satisfying. Somehow, she stands back. She finds herself judging people, even though she doesn't really feel that she wants to be a judgmental person. It doesn't feel like a choice so much as a temperament. As you help her clarify things, she realizes that she doesn't really trust people. You have explained to her that the best bad code examples are the ones that are irrational, and you help her come up with the bad code of her mistrust, which is pretty basic: *"I can't trust anyone."* She sees that it make sense that she would have various ways of keeping her distance from people if she can't trust them. Judging them helps her maintain that distance and refrain from the risks that trust entails.

Good Code:

The earliest memories that she has in connection with not trusting people were from her childhood. She has always been a pretty independent thinker, but her parents were very religious and they judged her thinking, which was anything but doctrinaire.

This leads you to think that her good code will have to do with being able to trust her judgement about people, and being able to fully own the fact that she is an adult and no longer under the scrutiny of her parents. As you help her come up with the good code that she would like to take the place of her bad code, it seems too simple to just say, *"I can trust people."* After all, she is a skeptical person, and she knows that you can't trust everyone. Perhaps, you say, it should be something like, *"I can trust myself to create meaningful relationships."* This touches something in her, because it brings her closer to the grief that she has buried regarding the betrayal of her childhood by her very rigid parents. She decides that this is pretty good, and she understands that she can refine this as she goes along. You like this good code, because it represents success and flexibility.

Code Triggers:

You have her look back over her timeline and identify some of the more recent events that have triggered her tendency to distance and be judgmental. She realizes that part of the pattern includes her having difficulty expressing her more vulnerable feelings from a powerful place. This results in her rarely exposing herself. This has really affected her primary relationship, in particular. You make a mental note that this is an important skill that she will need to learn in order to really make her work with you translate into a better life. You'll certainly want to have her practice the *Vision Communication Protocol* from this book. The triggers that she comes up with don't seem to have much of a theme. As she said before, it's more like a state of mind that she carries with her into most situations. But she is most judgmental of people she does not know very well, and of people who are making bad judgments, especially if they are inconsiderate toward her. But it isn't being judgmental that is the problem so much as being preoccupied with judging people and carrying around a feeling of distance from people that is salted with mistrust.

Source Event: Now you have her go back through her timeline and identify the source event. You might use timeline visualization for this. As she thinks back through her life, she gets to her earliest memory of feeling a lack of trust. She realizes that the ongoing patter of judcgmentality in her own mind is what she absorbed from her parents. She is carrying on the reality that she grew up in. But she is able to remember a harsh interaction with her mother that left a strong impression when she was very young and starting to ask too many questions for her parents' comfort.

This is her earliest memory that has the themes of judcgmentality, mistrust, and betrayal. She was precocious and developed abstract thinking that her parents could not understand. As a child seeking the truth, her trust was fundamentally violated.

Echo Events:

Your client sees that there are many situations that came along after this, though none of them had a strong impact. The strongest echo event happened when she was a teenager, and realized how important it was to her to get out on her own. She didn't just need this for her independence, but for her own sanity. At least it felt that way to her.

Future Success: She defines future success, so far as this issue is concerned, with being at peace around people, and appreciating her own power and ability to exercise realistic judgment about others. A lot of it is just about accepting the truth that she has good judgment about people. She describes feeling confident and at peace in various situations. She imagines how she would be flexible and not distracted by people who are inconsiderate or quirky.

Reprocessing: Knowing all this, you are in a good position to reprocess the source event. You will target this, along with her feelings of judgment, betrayal, and insecurity. As you go, you will bring up the bad code and target that as well. If the process is simple, you will find that the bad code has less and less power, and the good code makes more and more sense at a gut level. Unless you have training and supervised experience in reprocessing and cognitive work, you will want to only do reprocessing with situations that do not involve serious dysfunction, substance abuse, or dissociation.

Working With the Time Line

An NLP practitioner familiar with Time Line Therapy ™ will find countless ways to integrate reprocessing into this work. In fact, they will probably recognize ways that it is already in play and can be enhanced.

> The visualization of the time line that occurs at the same time as more conscious, verbal processing creates a kind of bilateral stimulus that promotes a reprocessing state.

We believe this is a key reason that Time Line Therapy ™ works for so many people. From the reprocessing to the timeline work: Let's say that you have directly reprocessed an issue. You may have gotten to it in doing timeline work, or it may have been a presenting problem. You can do timeline work from this point through means such as sophisticated future pacing.

From Timeline Work Into Reprocessing:

You can travel back into the timeline to find additional echo events. In Time Line Therapy ™, *source* and *echo* events are addressed through means such as bringing in the client's adult self to contact the child, or imagining resources being in place. An alternative is to directly do reprocessing, and then see what additional timeline methods are necessary. This can greatly expedite timeline work and make it more consistently effective with a broader range of clients.

More Integration With Cognitions:

Now that you know how negative cognitions work in reprocessing, you can integrate this into timeline work. You can identify how a negative (or limiting) cognition has played out through the timeline and recalibrate the timeline as a result of reprocessing that allows the client to fully accept a positive cognition. As you help the client undo their *bad code*, you need to know how powerful it is. You can ask the client to tell you, on a scale of one to ten, how true the code seems.

> You must make sure that the client understands that you are talking about how true it feels.

They must not rate it by how logical it is. You are, after all, working with illogical code. But you can do the same with *good code*. When the client begins working with good code, they will tell you that, although they understand that it is true, it doesn't "feel" very true. When they think of it, something at gut level signals them that they cannot completely accept it on a feeling level. Again, they can help you know where things are by rating its gut level power on a scale of one to ten. You can even focus your targeting more effectively by having them target the feeling between this rating and a ten. If they only give it a six, what are the feelings and impressions that are holding it down to that level? Target those for reprocessing.

Tracking and Processing Source Event Power:

The source event is disturbing in some way or ways. Ask the client what is most disturbing or upsetting about it. That is what you target. To track the power of the source event, ask them to rate those disturbing feelings on a scale of one to ten. When reprocessing is working, the number will go down.

As you'll recall, we have talked about identifying feelings and helping the client cooperate with processes through "economy of speech." Those elements are very helpful with reprocessing.

Challenges to Reprocessing

Reprocessing is a deep subject, so we really cannot cover every aspect in depth, but we do need to go over some challenges that can come up. The most common problems that come up are these:

1) The client does not get a reduction in the power of the source event or bad code.

2) They do not get an increase in the power of the good code.

3) Or they may have progress, but end up cycling through similar material, showing that they are not really reprocessing it and getting anywhere.

When these problems come up, these are common issues to address:

1) The client needs work with will prepare them to tolerate more advanced work. Clients with severe childhood trauma or dissociation usually need this. Specialized treatment should be recommended.

2) You need additional training or supervision.

3) The client needs a referral to a specialist

4) You need to improvise with your other NLP skills to address the issues that are challenging the reprocessing.

5) You need a breakthrough concept. This can be a better target, a better formulation of the positive and negative cognitions, or some other way to break out of your current paradigm.

Post-Mystical Hyper-Structuralism

As you know, the meta-model helps us escape mental traps that limit or distort reality. They include deletions and generalizations. While we are incapable to perceiving everything all at once, we must be on guard against destructive distortions that result in bad outcomes.

A great deal has been written on the meta-model; however, the solutions shown often have the quality of interrogation or sarcasm. Fortunately, modeling of great therapists provides us with endless examples of therapeutic responses to meta-model violations.

We are going to show you four levels at which you can respond to meta-model violations.

1) **Original:** This is typical of what you might find in a old NLP training manual.

2) **Motive:** This takes things up a notch by focusing on the statement from a more dynamic vantage point.

3) **Meta:** This goes a level higher, looking at the system dynamic.

4) **Moment:** This takes the bull by the horns. It subsumes each of the preceding levels and adds an authoritative, therapeutic leadership position. The moment response starts with a kind of

problem statement that serves as a good catapult for being incisive and prescriptive, and ends with one or more recommendations.

In real life, there might be more back and forth in order to maintain rapport and develop agreement.

In these examples, you'll see a somewhat more truncated version. There is some *Ericksonian* influence in that the moment responses tend to frame the situation in the here and now, bringing up an aspect in the environment or situation that is undeniably true and that may foster a mild trance effect, and in that they imply that something is happening as though what is to be recommended is actually somehow foreordained.

As much as possible, these moment responses should do "*utilization*," (the Ericksonian propensity for gaining value from things that appear symptomatic or intractable). The term "moment" is used because:

1) A *moment* in history is a phrase that intends to capture the key dynamics of a given time;

2) The response treats the moment as a sort of vortex of dynamics that are to be utilized

to create a tipping point in which the situation will qualitatively change.

We will go through these levels from several *vantage* points or "*filters*." We'll go through each of the four levels for each filter. They include the following.

1) Action:

A focus on actions taken by individuals, questioning their legitimacy, and substituting something more generative.

2) Context:

A focus on the situation, questioning it's integrity, and providing a more supportive situation.

3) Originator:

A focus on the person making the judgment or meta-model violation, and on questioning their authority to do so. This focus especially can provide an authoritative, responsible approach toward achieving a good outcome.

4) Source:

A look backward through the dynamics to view causes and to question related assumptions. It is especially good for establishing alternatives that will change the pattern for the better.

5) Essence:

> Viewing the meta-model violation in terms of how it characterizes the essence of a person or situation. It questions the legitimacy of the oversimplification and generates an expanded view.

Notice how, as you read the responses, the lower-level ones may have a seductive appeal because of their "gotcha" sarcasm.

Notice how this is a kind of *hook* within you that could be holding you back from a more productive and stress-reducing response. Imagine having the most enlightened leadership spontaneously emerge from you in a confident and authoritative, yet spontaneous fashion. Imagine this happening with ease and a sense of enjoyable mastery. *Anchor this state, and activate it when you read each of the "moment" responses.*

Five Examples: Responding to Deletions

What follows are the examples promised in the previous section:

Notice how each response might have a function, depending on what's going on. Each response is to the meta-model violation *"He's just a failure."* You are responding to a father whose son is 28 and has some kind of impairment that is preventing him from experiencing success that you might expect from him. He's fairly bright. The family hasn't quite come to terms with the fact that there is impairment, so they're still struggling with him and moralizing.

Calling the son a failure is a deletion in meta-model terms. As you'll recall deletions *omit* important information. More specifically, this is the "poorly specified adjective" form of deletion, in which a word is essentially meaningless without further information and operationalization. It is used as a noun here, but functions as an adjective by being used as a reified statement of essence.

In our minds, we'll translate the phrase into, "He is failure-essenced," or "failure-destined." Here are the responses, through each of the four filters and levels described above.

The Action Filter

Original Action: What exactly does he do that means he is a failure?

Motive-Action: Then he will never succeed?

Meta-Action: Judging him helps you express your frustration, yes?

Moment-Action: To judge a person completely, we must consider all of their abilities, not just their errors, whatever they may be, especially when we will make such a tremendous difference in their life. We have gathered from our discussions the following strengths or abilities, and even some good examples. We even have ways to leverage each of them into future successes...

Note that this response uses judgmental language as a part of pacing the kind of person who would judge a family member as being merely a failure. This kind of thing helps you work in more ideas without them closing their mind.

The Intention Filter

Original Intention: Which of his choices make him a failure?

Motive-Intention: How would you say his judgment fails him?

Meta-Intention: Getting everyone to simplify him makes him easier to defeat, doesn't it?

Moment-Intention: It seems that his successful behaviors are not yet consistently well orchestrated. We think he's a late-bloomer. We know of three ways that we can make him more of an asset to the family...

The Context Filter

Original Context: What exactly made him into a failure?

Motive-Context: So this situation defines him forever?

Meta-Context: You can conserve your family's resources by writing him off, we suppose.

Moment-Context: We can see three ways that the situation set him up to fail, despite his strengths. We now realize that he has some specific problems, but here are the obstacles that we can get out of his way...

The Originator Filter

Original Originator (speaker): What has given you the authority to define him?

Motive-Originator: You know enough about him to say that nothing else characterizes him as well as failure does?

Meta-Originator: The way your body language becomes so powerful, I imagine that calling him a failure is a real rush for you.

Moment-Originator: These disappointments are so strong for you, and with all the past disappointments before him, we would never expect you to trust him right now. It will take a lot of willingness to experiment, just to try out some of the things I'll begin suggesting today.

The Source Filter

Original Source: What caused him to be a failure? What makes it his fault, exactly?

Motive-Source: So his parents and teachers failed, and he is their failure?

Meta-Source: By not looking at the situation around him, you have avoided rocking the boat, haven't you?

Moment-Source: When this situation comes up again, there will have to be some new things going on so that we are taking charge to make a difference in his life. Specifically, we can start with...

The Essence Filter

Original Essence: How exactly can you tell that failure is his essence or nature?

Motive-Essence: Then his most salient property is that of failure. Nothing about him is as important?

Meta-Essence: Seeing one thing as the essence of a person gives you a more stable, predictable world to live in, doesn't it?

Moment-Essence: This failure aspect of him is so prominent right now in our minds, we'll have to make some changes so that our biases don't condemn him to a self-fulfilling prophecy, and no matter how much he might cooperate with that pattern.

Presuppositions

Presuppositions are, in general, the underlying assumptions of a system. To fully comprehend NLP, one must first gain a thorough understanding of its underlying assumptions. Even if the statement itself is not necessarily true, the cultivation of a useful result is accomplished.

> Or to put it another way, we act as if these statements are "facts" solely for the purpose of bringing us one step closer to our desired outcomes.

As an example, suppose you want to have a strong and loving relationship with your children. You choose to not get upset by your teenage son's recent outburst, instead offering support, unconditional love, and patience, acting on the assumption (presupposing) that we are more than our behavior (#7).

You seek to understand the deep structure that has contributed to the inappropriate behavior, and instead of reflexive conflict, you show empathy and care, knowing that your son's rudeness was a temporary reaction initiated because it was the most useful (#8) in that specific context (#9). Remembering that your reaction to his outburst is critical (# 11 and # 12), you take a step back and say, "You have the right to be angry, and I am here to listen whenever you are willing to talk to me about it." Compare that to yelling at him, "Stop acting like a child! You're grounded! Now go to your room!"

The NLP Presuppositions

1. The map is not the territory.

2. People respond according to their internal maps.

3. Meaning operates context-dependently.

4. The mind and-body affect each other.

5. Individual skills function by the development and sequencing of rep systems.

6. We respect each person's model of the world.

7. Person and behavior describe different phenomena. We are more than our behavior.

8. Every behavior has utility and usefulness–in some context.

9. We evaluate behavior and change in terms of context and ecology.

10. We cannot not communicate.

11. The way we communicate affects perception and reception.

12. The meaning of communication lies in the response you get.

13. The person who sets the frame for the communication controls the outcome.

14. There is no failure, only feedback.

15. The person with the most flexibility exercises the most influence within the system.

16. Resistance indicates a lack of rapport.

17. People have the internal resources they need to succeed.

18. Humans have the ability to experience one-trial learning.

19. All communication should increase choice.

20. People make the best choices available to them when they act.

21. As response-able people, we can run our own brains and therefore choose our behavior.

Bibliography

An Insiders Guide to Sub Modalities, Will Macdonald and Richard Bandler, 1989

Beliefs: Pathways to Health and Wellbeing, Robert Dilts, Tim Hallbom, and Suzi Smith, 1990

Changing Belief Systems With NLP, Robert Dilts, 1990

Change Your Mind-And Keep the Change : Advanced NLP Encyclopedia of Systemic Neuro-Linguistic Programming and NLP New Coding, Robert B. Dilts and Judith A. Delozier, 2000

Frogs into Princes: Neuro Linguistic Programming, Richard Bandler, John Grinder, Steve Andreas, and John O. Srevens, 1979

From Coach to Awakener, Robert Dilts, 2003

Get the Life You Want: The Secrets to Quick and Lasting Life Change with Neuro-Linguistic Programming, Richard Bandler, 2008

Jay Haley On Milton H. Erickson, Jay Haley, 1993

Magic In Action, Richard Bandler, 1982Manage Yourself, Manage Your Life: Vital Nlp Techniques for Personal Well-Being and Professional Success, Ian McDermott and Ian Shircore, 1999

Modeling With NLP, Robert Dilts, 1998

My Voice Will Go With You: The Teaching Tales of Milton H. Erickson, M.D., Sidney Rosen, 1991Patterns of the Hypnotic Techniques of Milton H. Erickson, M.D. (Volume I), Richard; Grinder, John Bandler, 1975

Patterns of the Hypnotic Techniques of Milton H. Erickson, M.D., Vol. 2, John Grinder, Judith Delozier, and Richard Bandler, 1997

Reframing: Neuro-linguistic Programming and The Transformation of Meaning, Richard Bandler and John Grinder, 1982

Roots Of Neuro Linguistic Programming, Robert Dilts, 1983

Skills for the Future: Managing Creativity and Innovation, Robert Dilts and Gino Bonissone, 1993

Strategies of Genius, Volume Two, Robert Dilts, 1994

The Structure of Magic: A course About Language and Therapy (Structure of Magic), Richard Bandler and John Grinder, 1975

Tools of the Spirit, Robert Dilts and Robert McDonald, 1997

Uncommon Therapy: The Psychiatric Techniques of Milton H. Erickson, M.D., Jay Haley, 1993

"In Hollywood if you don't have a shrink, people think you're crazy."

— Johnny Carson

Printed in Dunstable, United Kingdom

81924594R00119